UNDER THE SEA

An Ocean Themed Adult Coloring Book

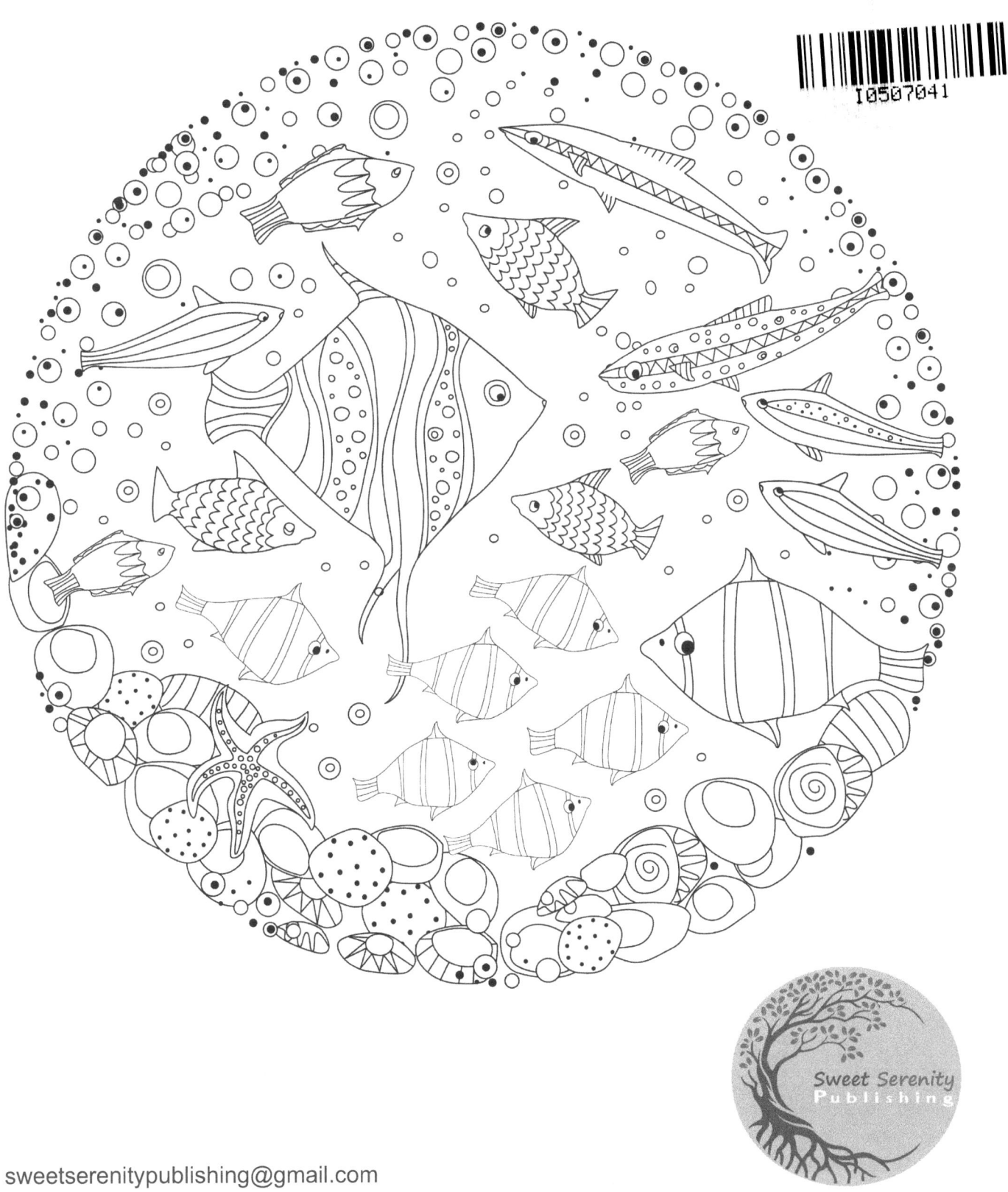

sweetserenitypublishing@gmail.com

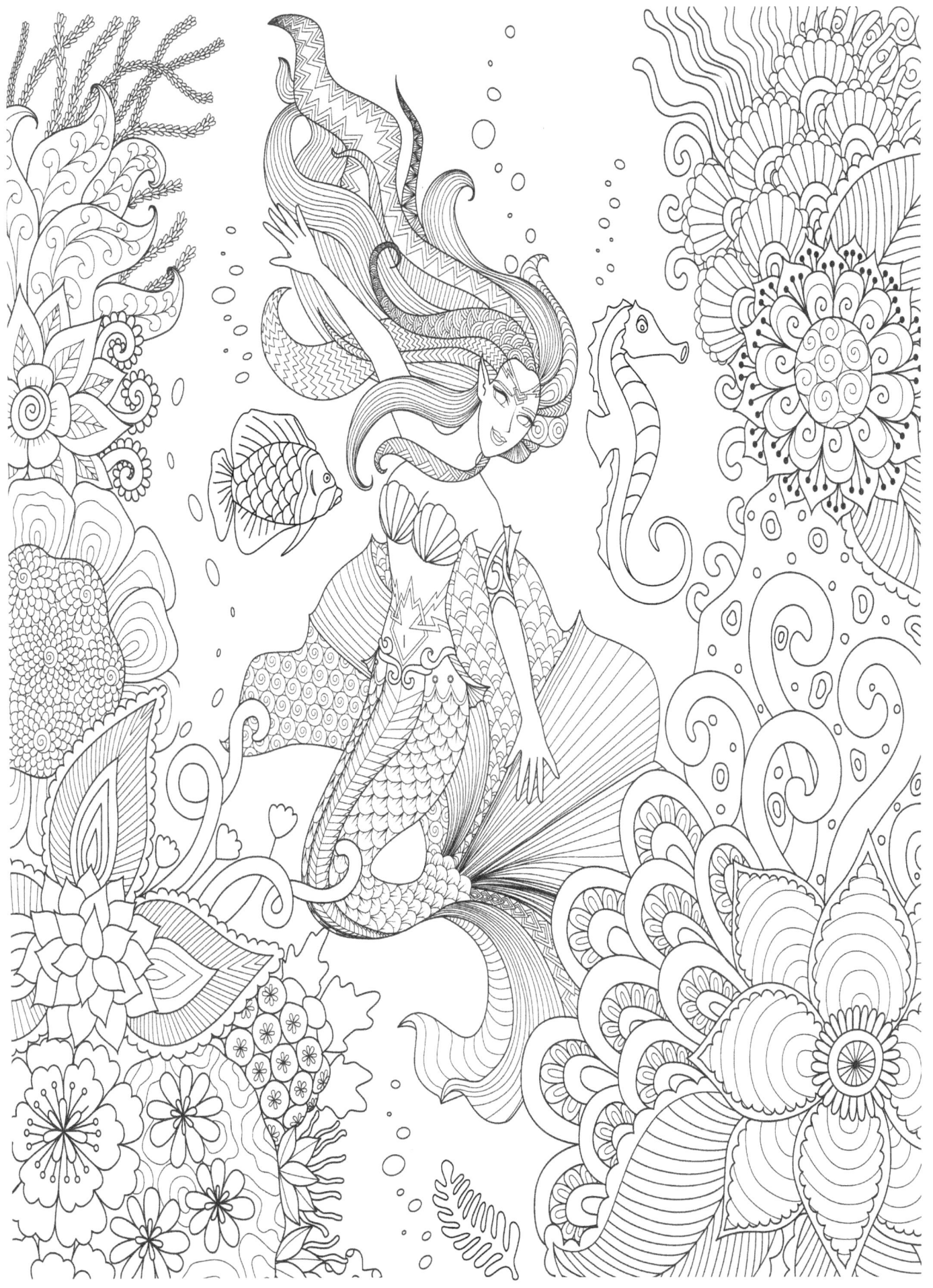

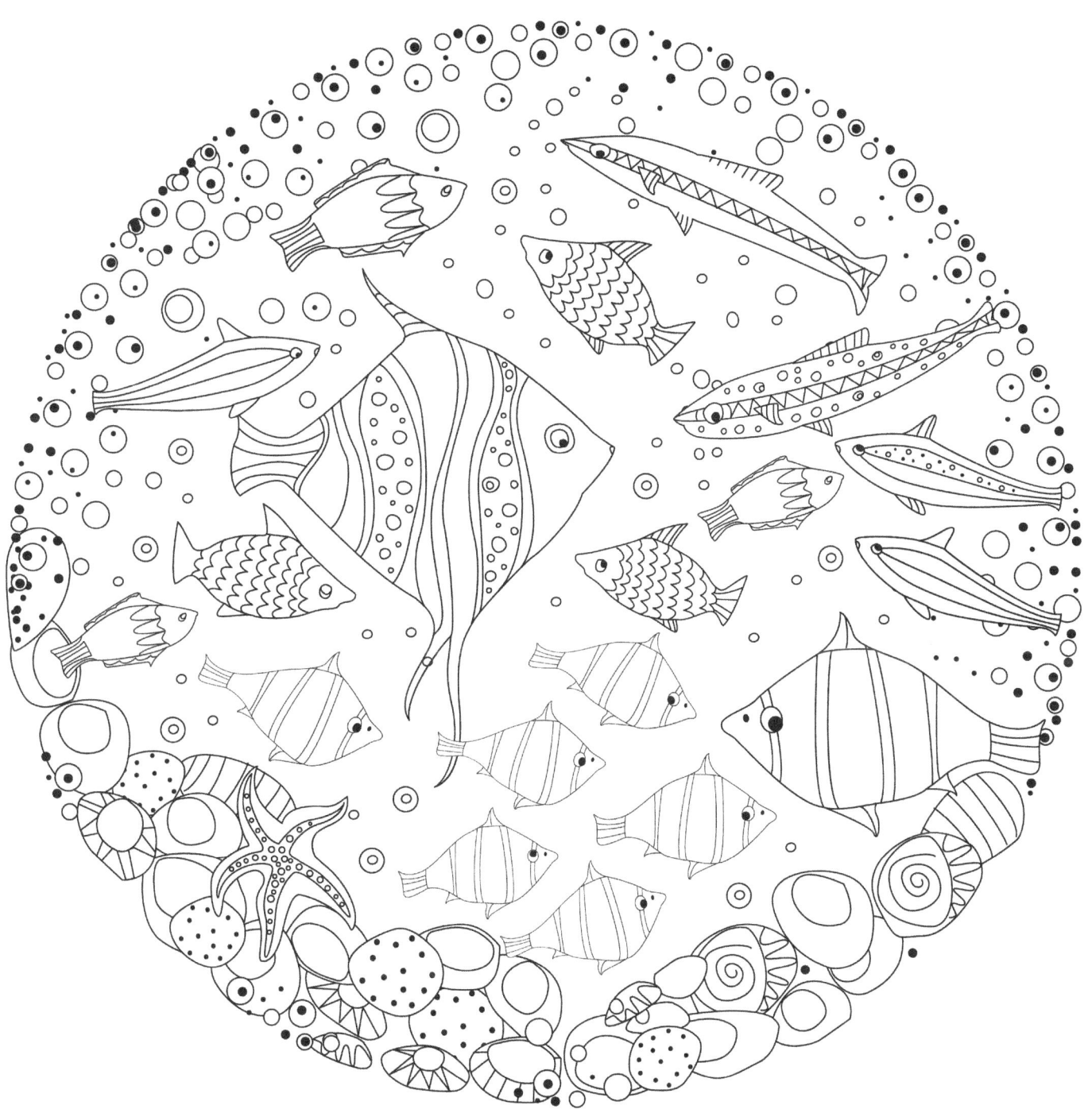

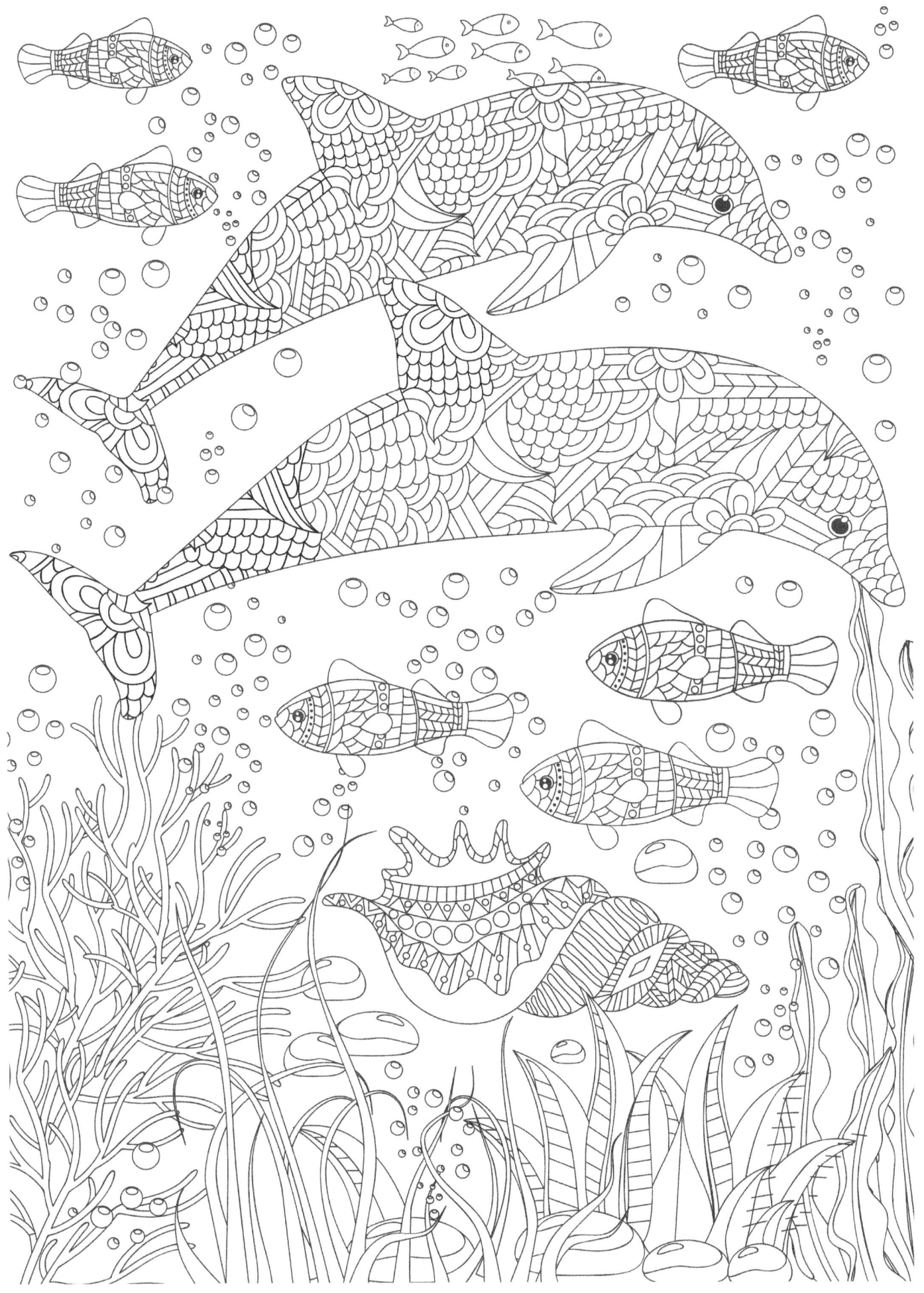

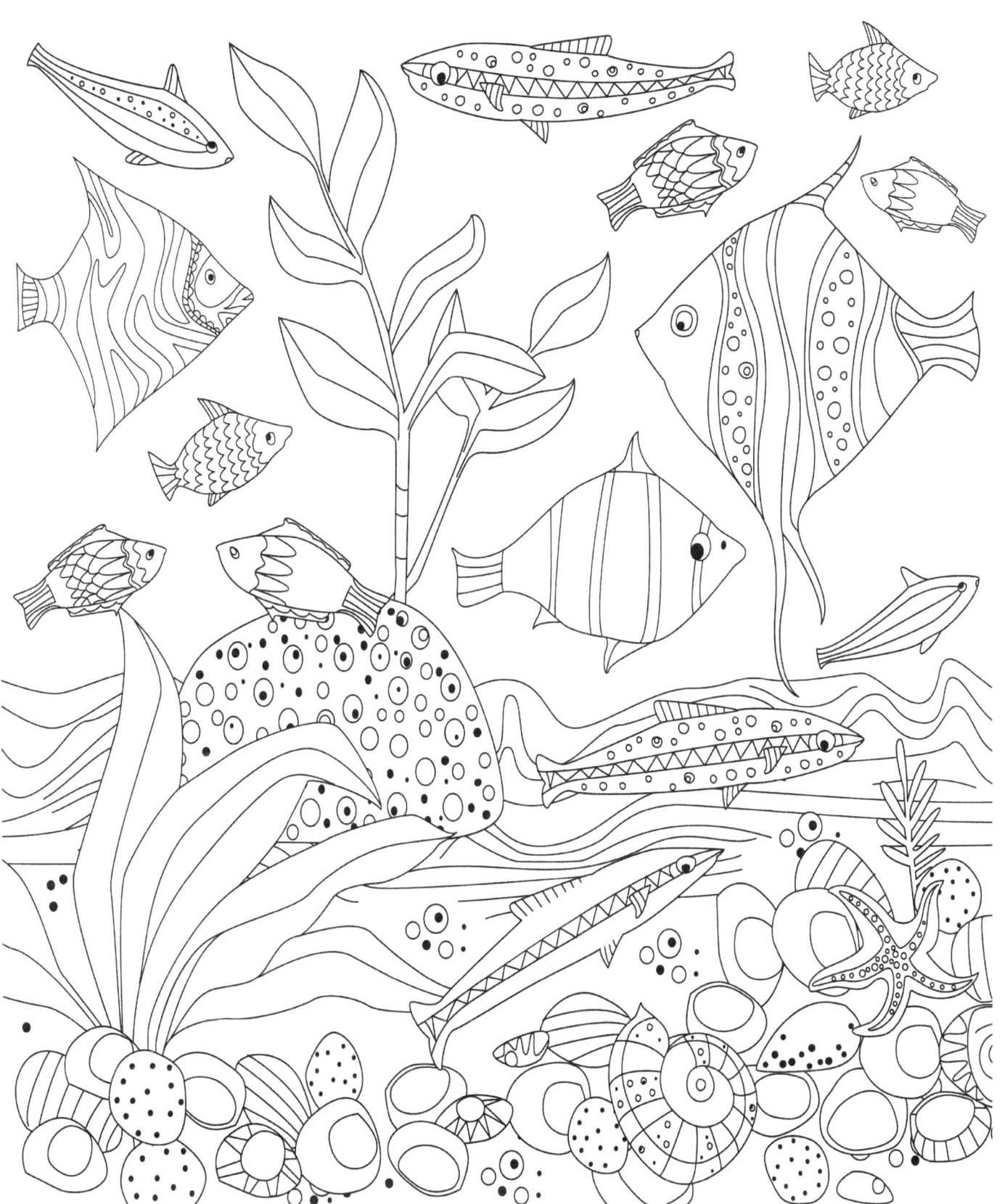

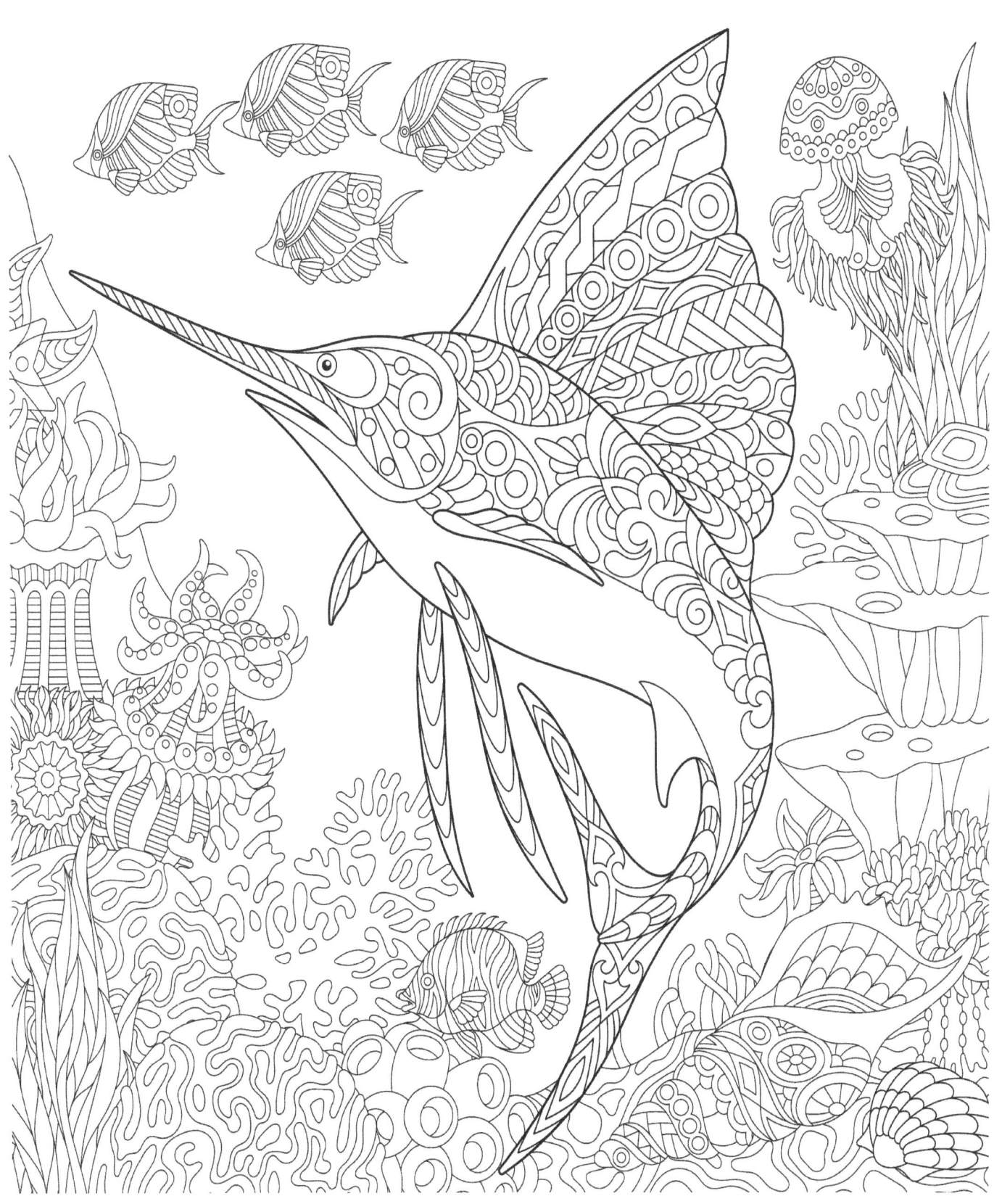

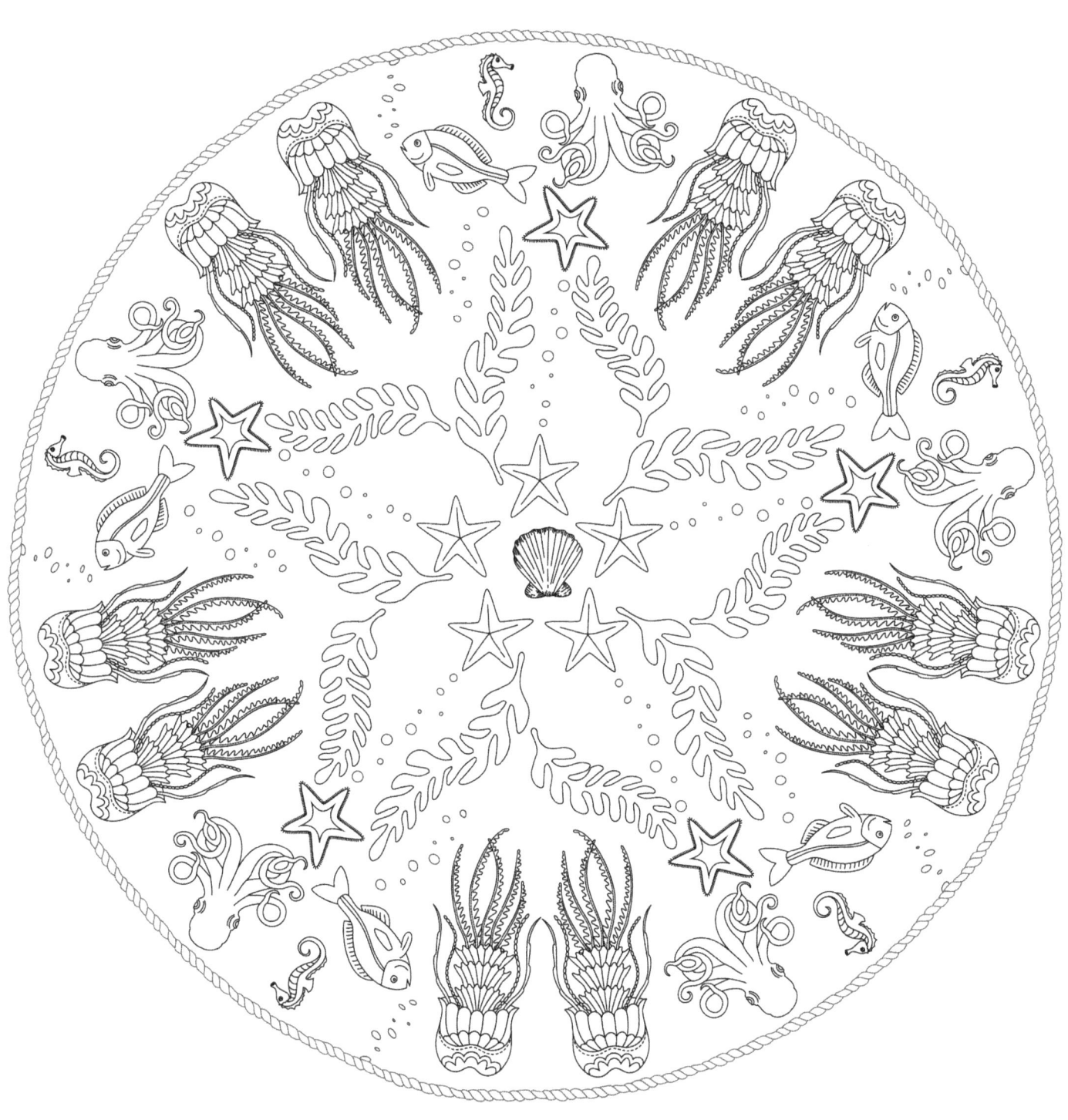

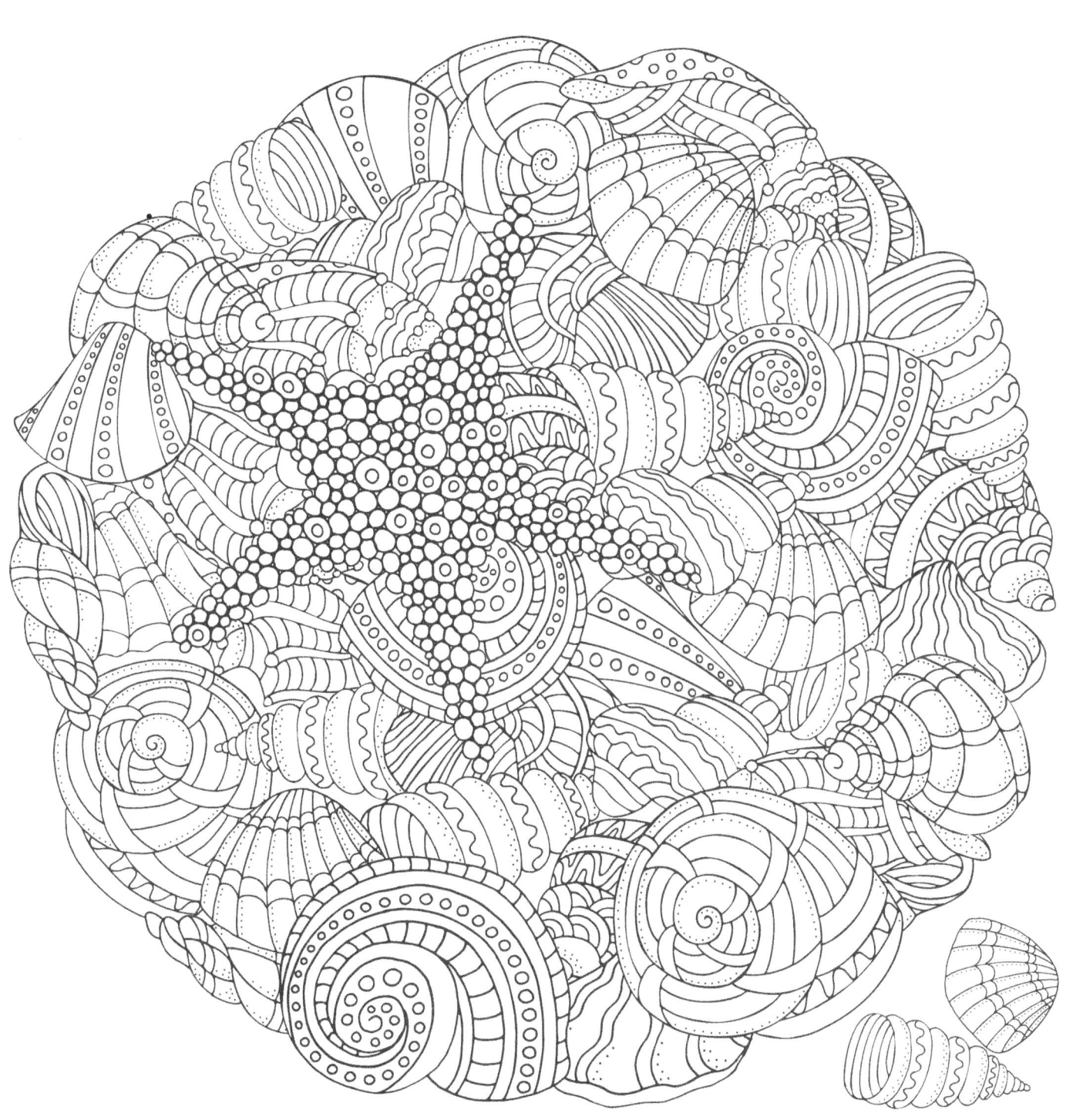

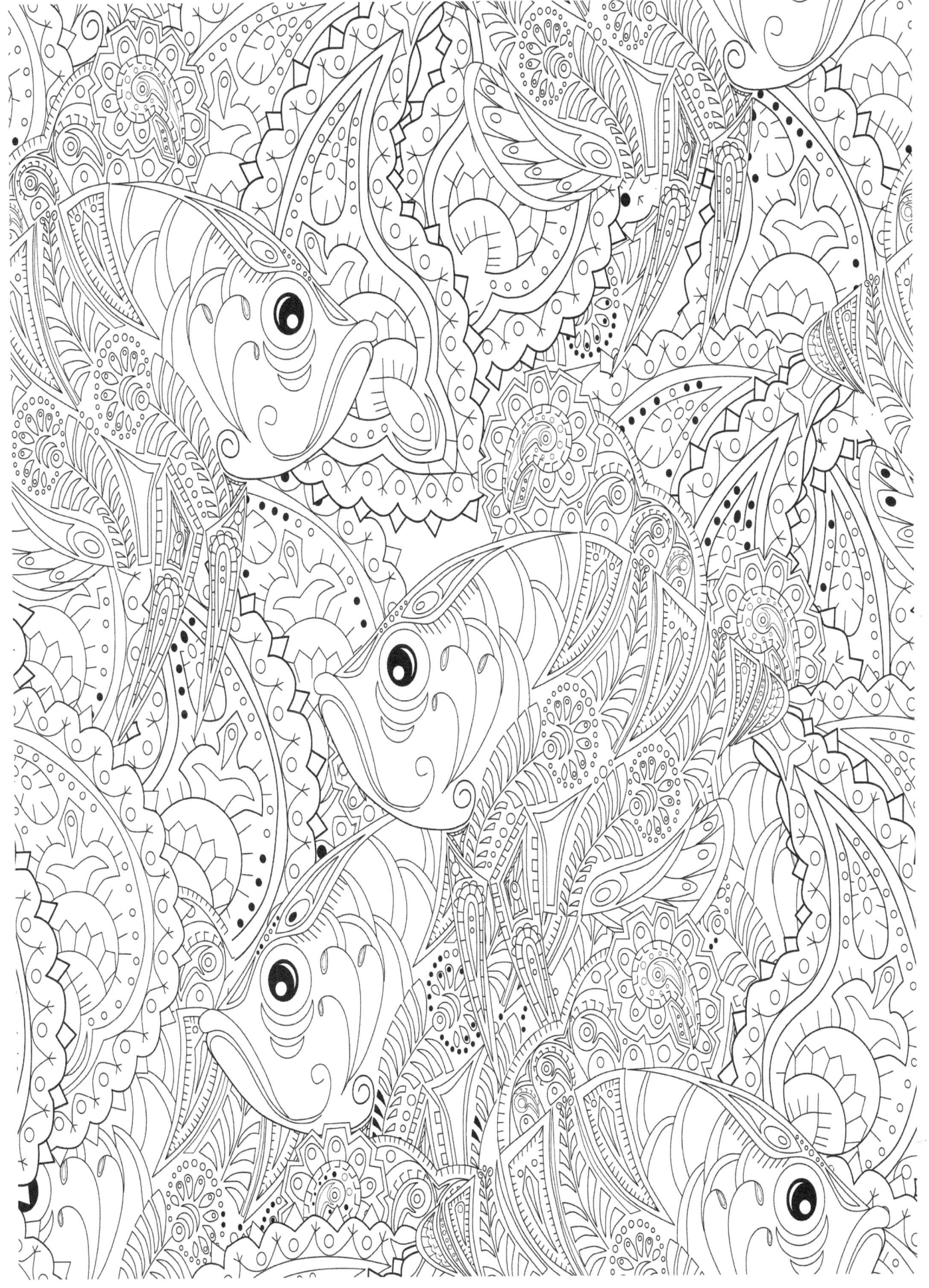

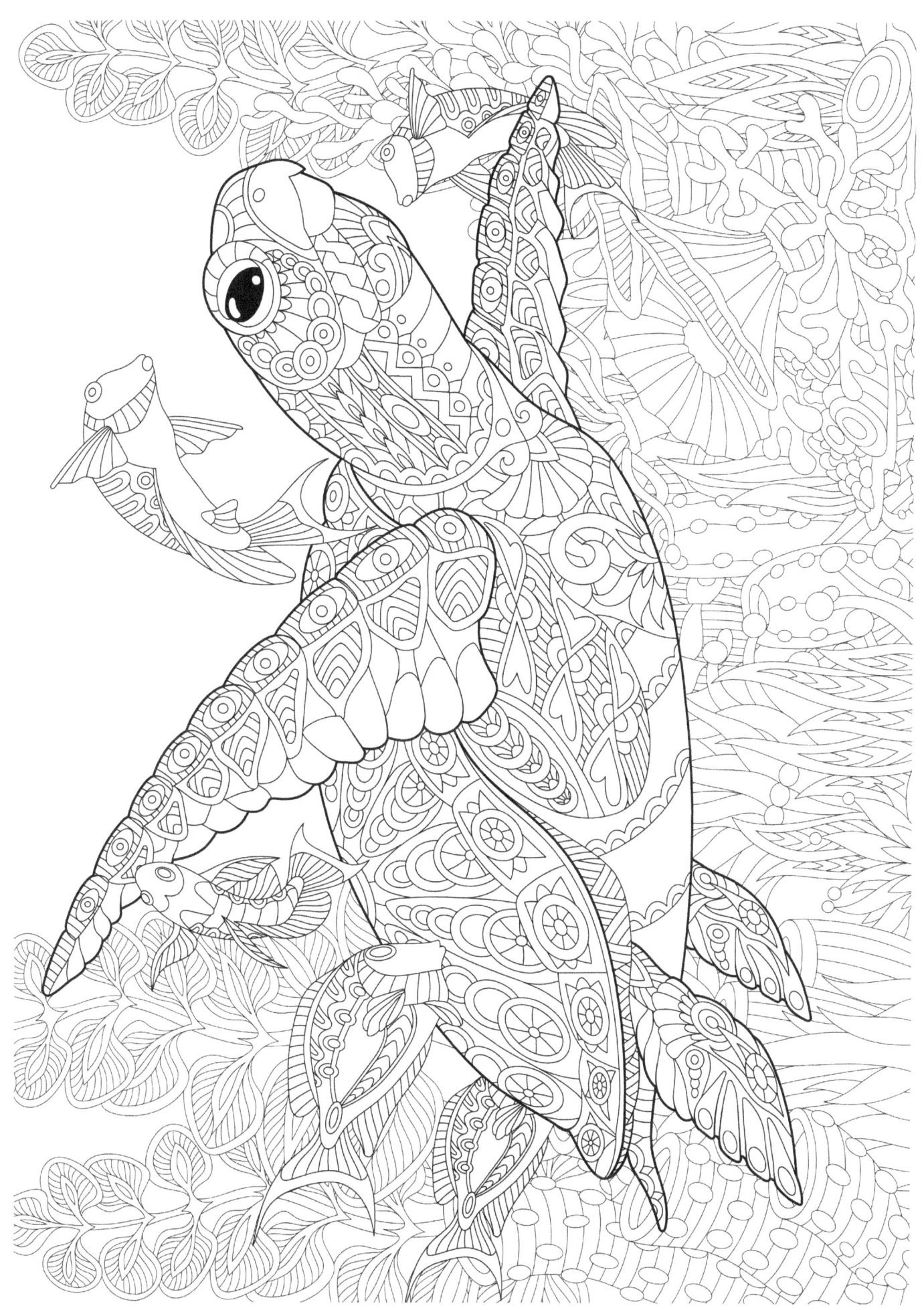

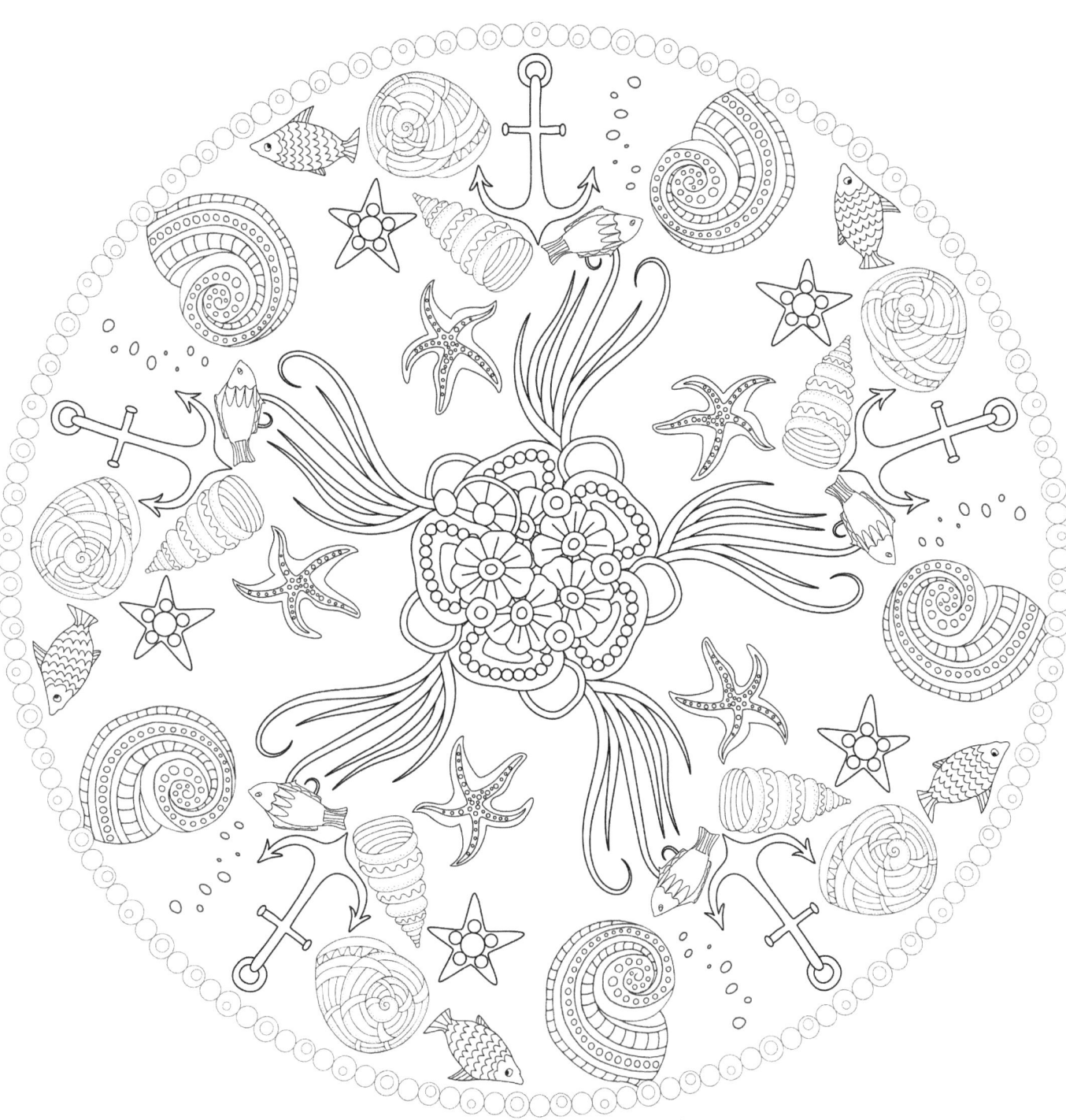

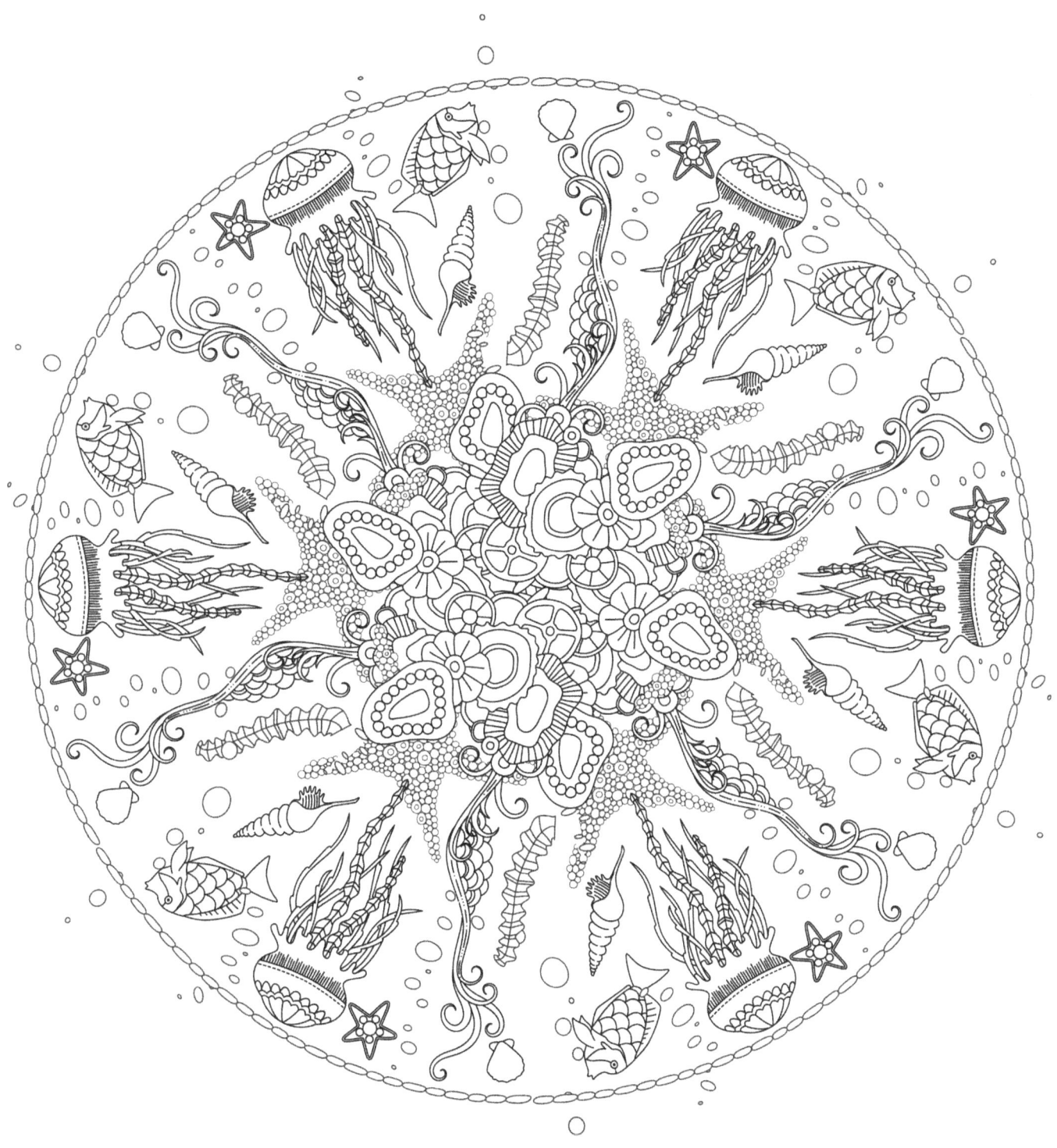

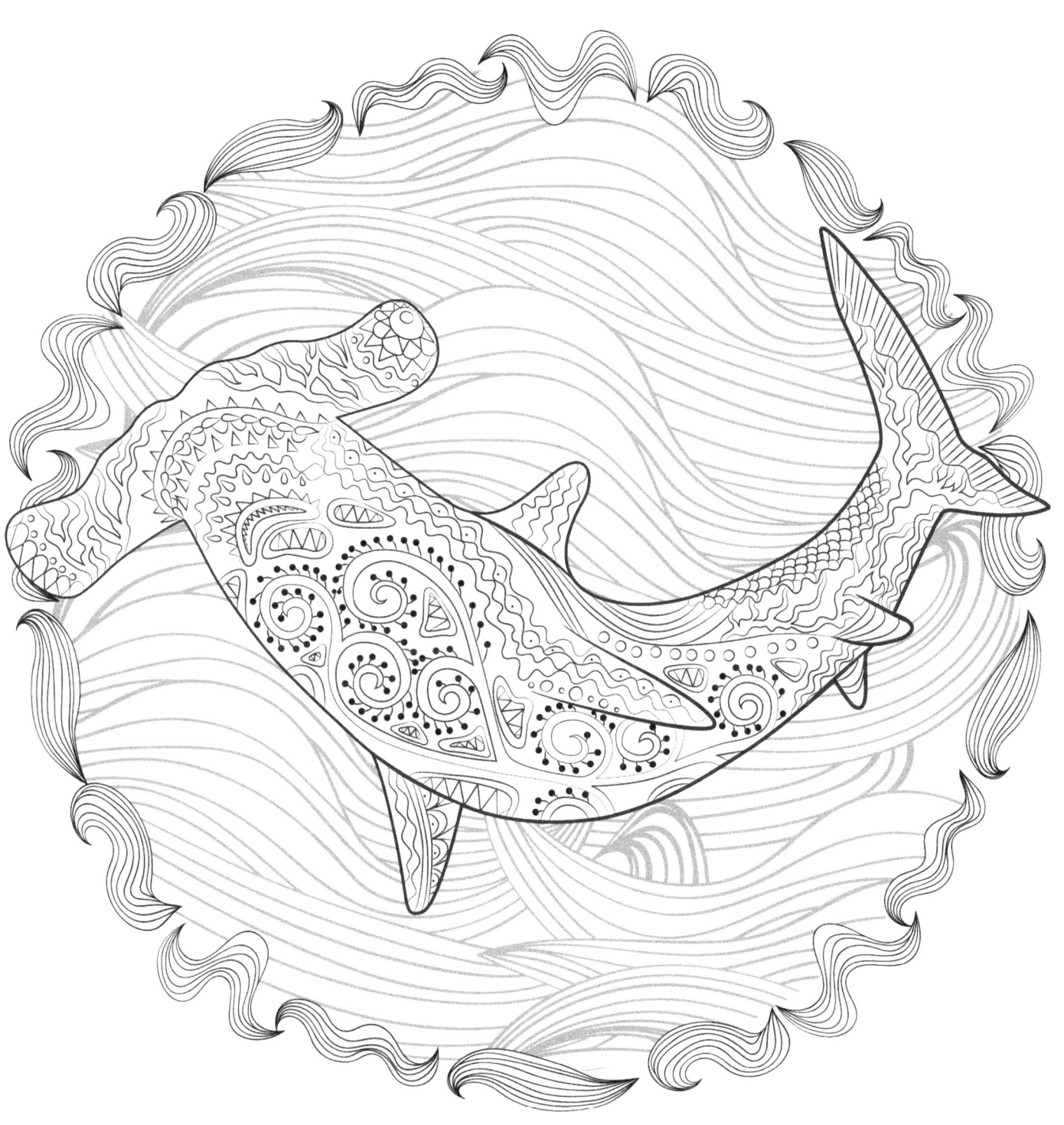

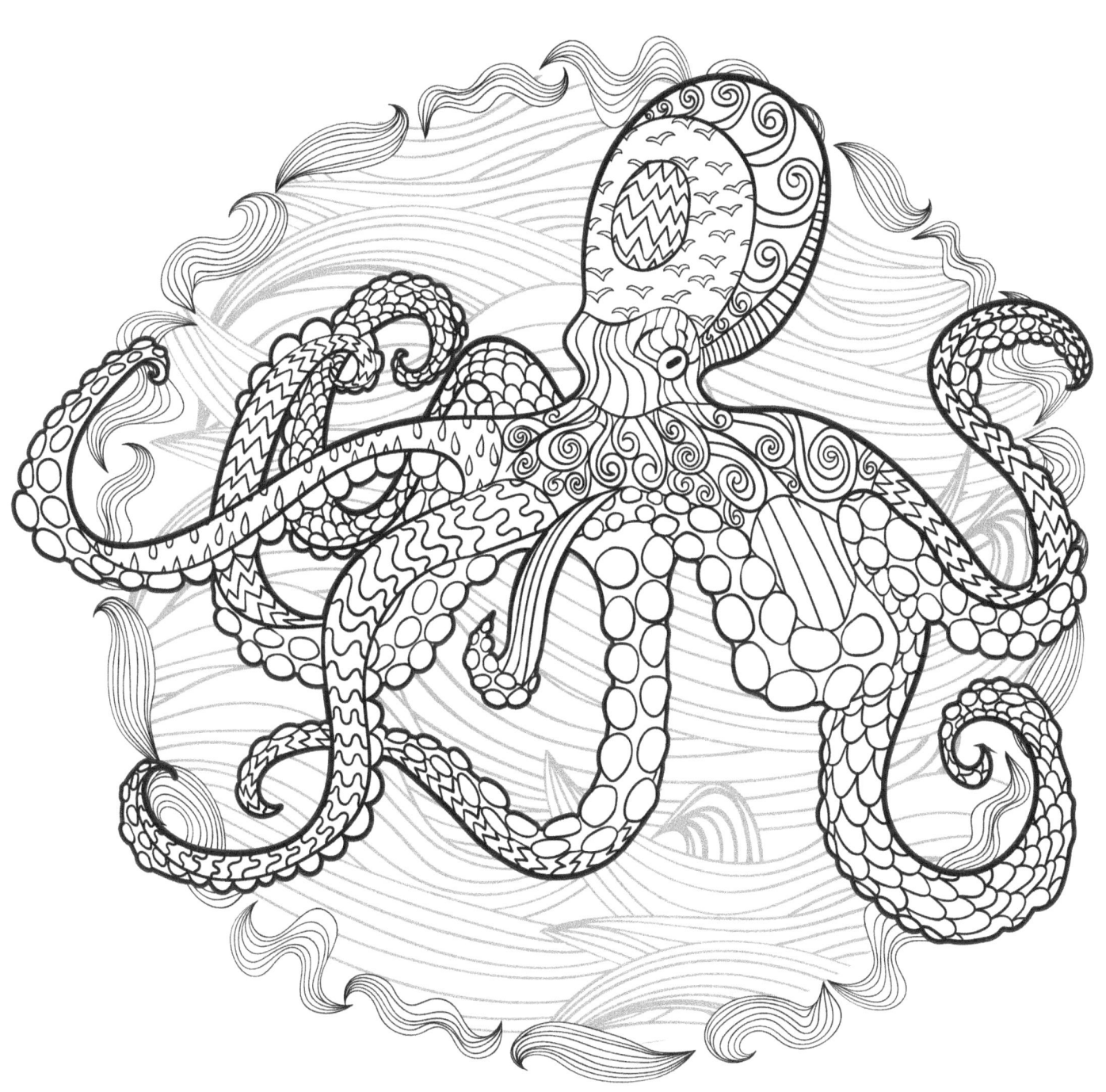

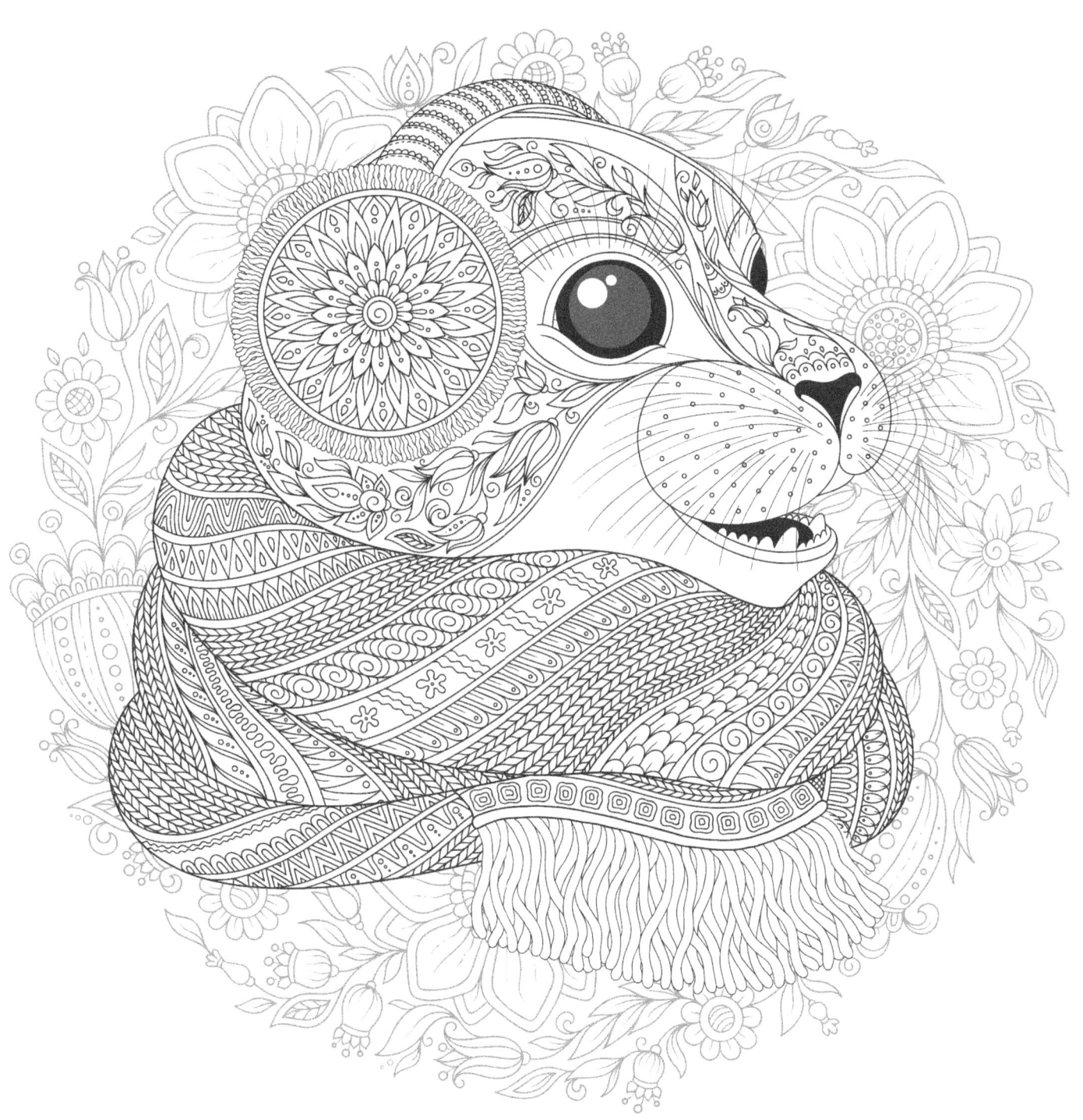

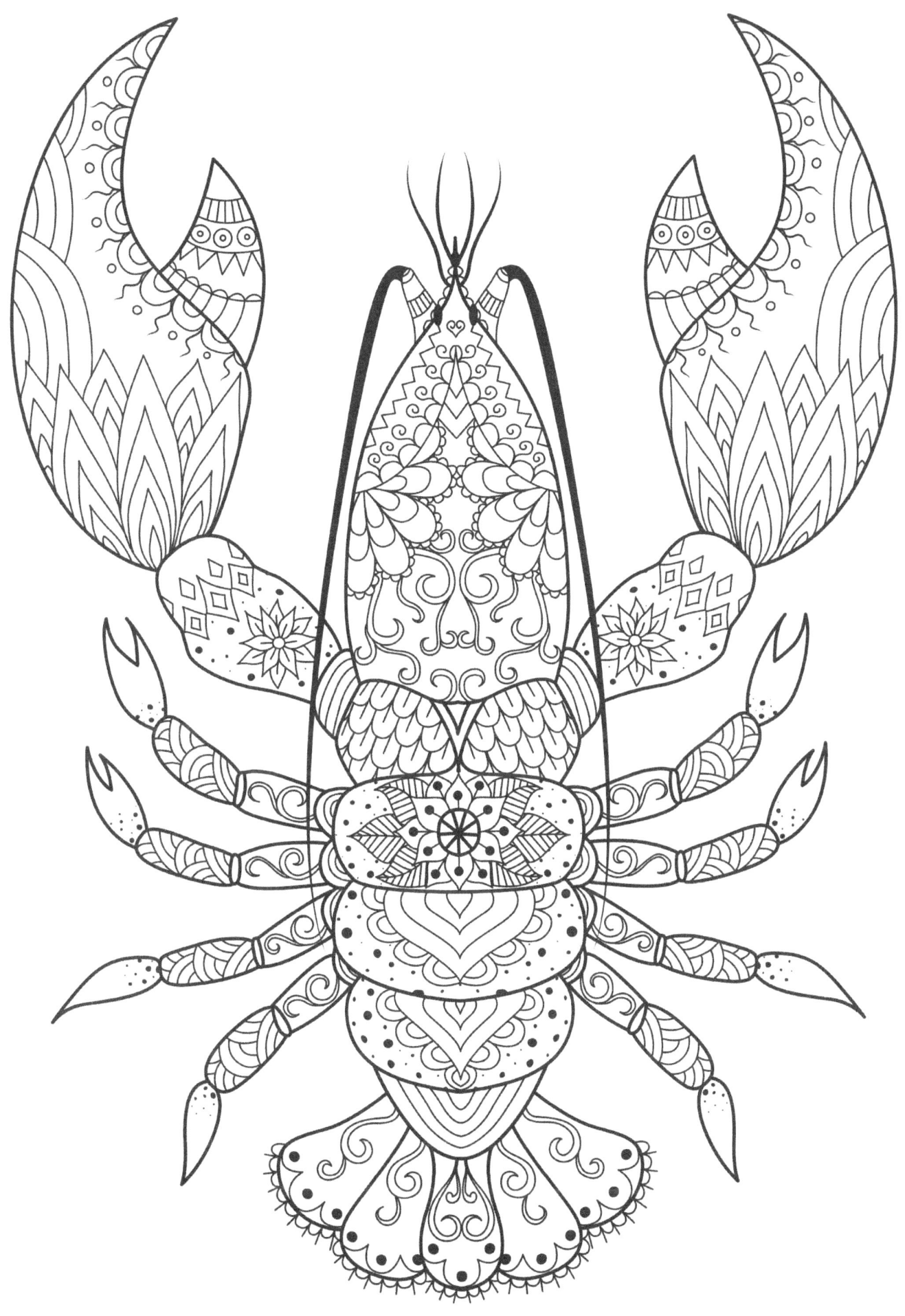

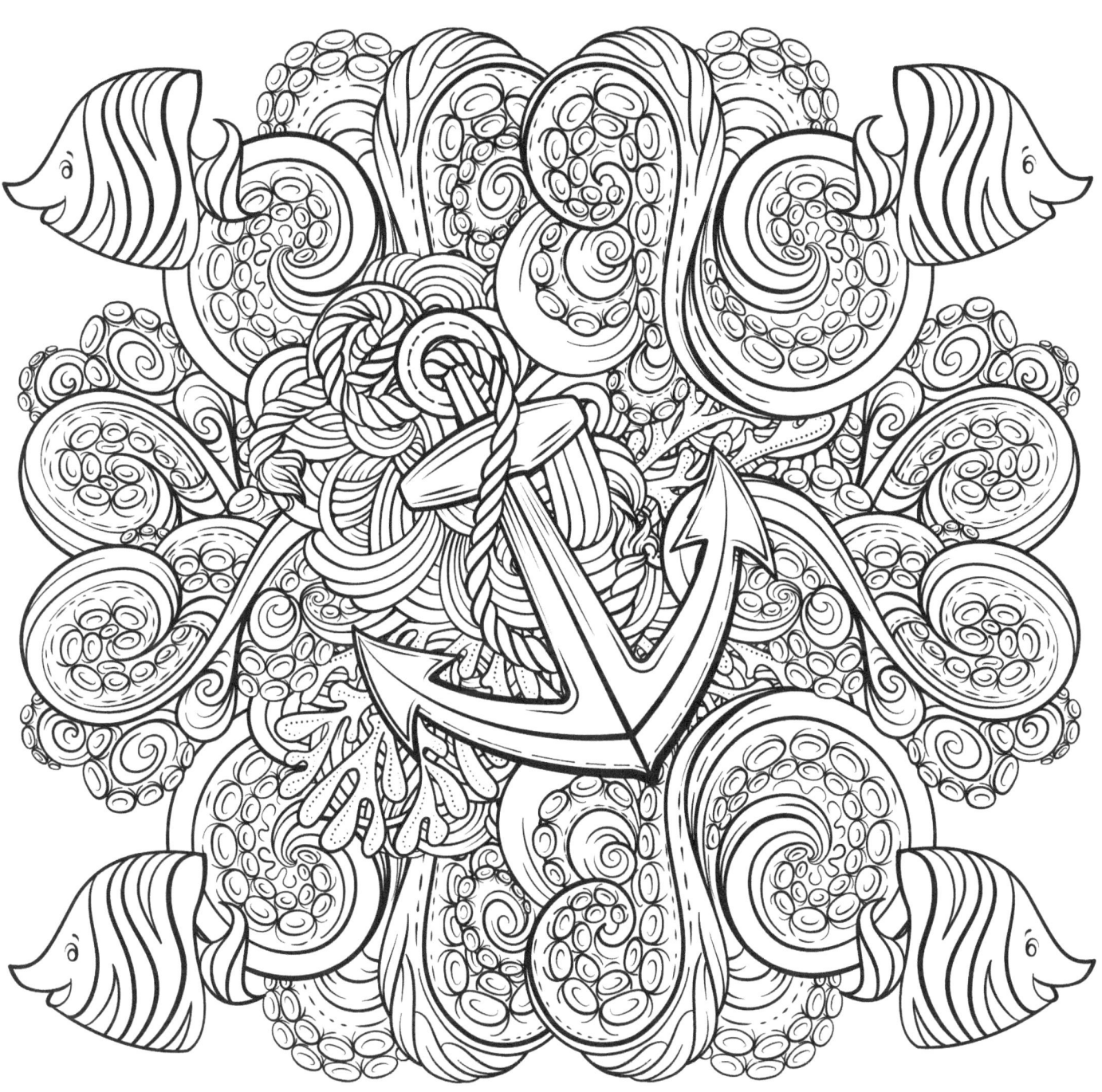

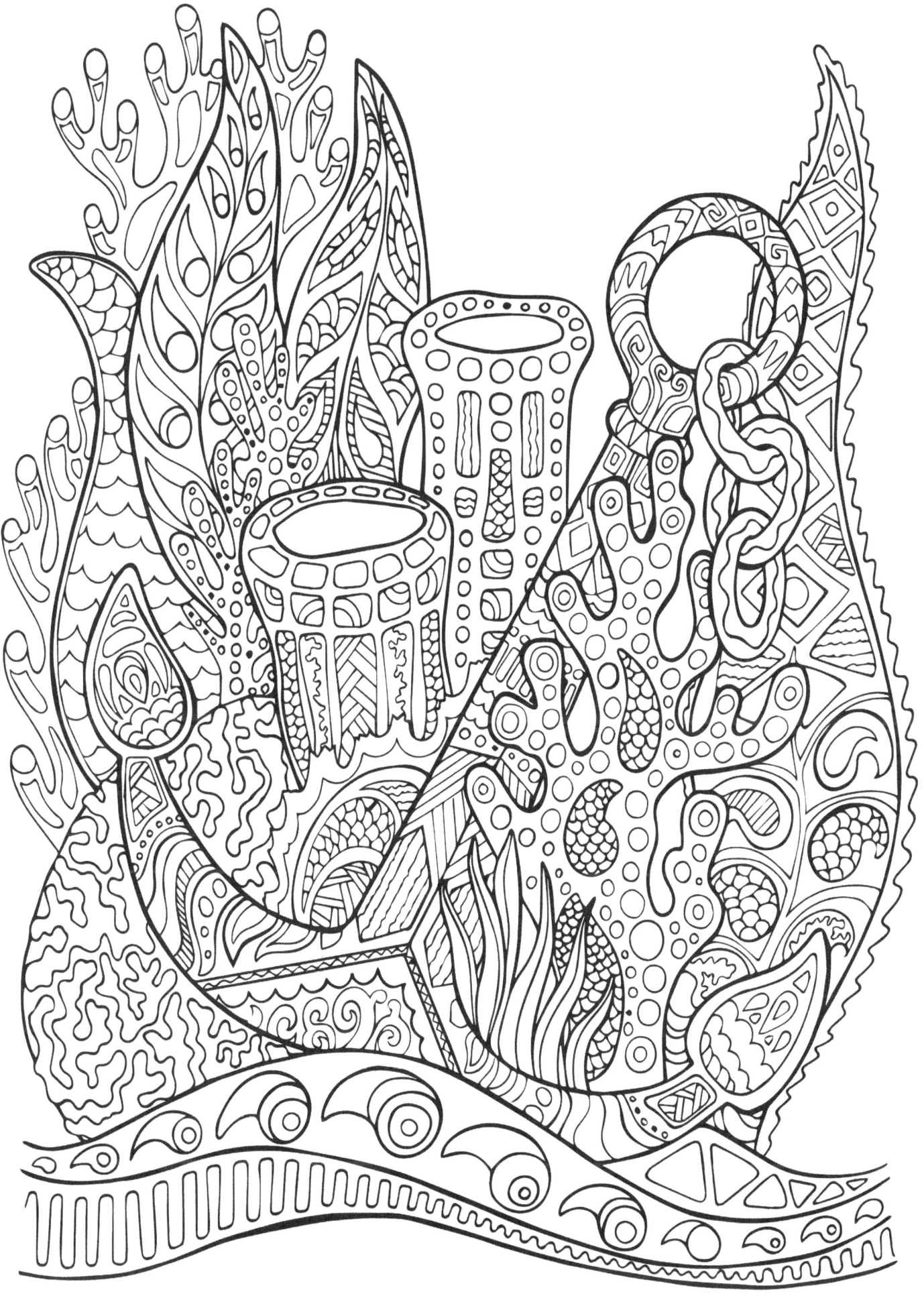

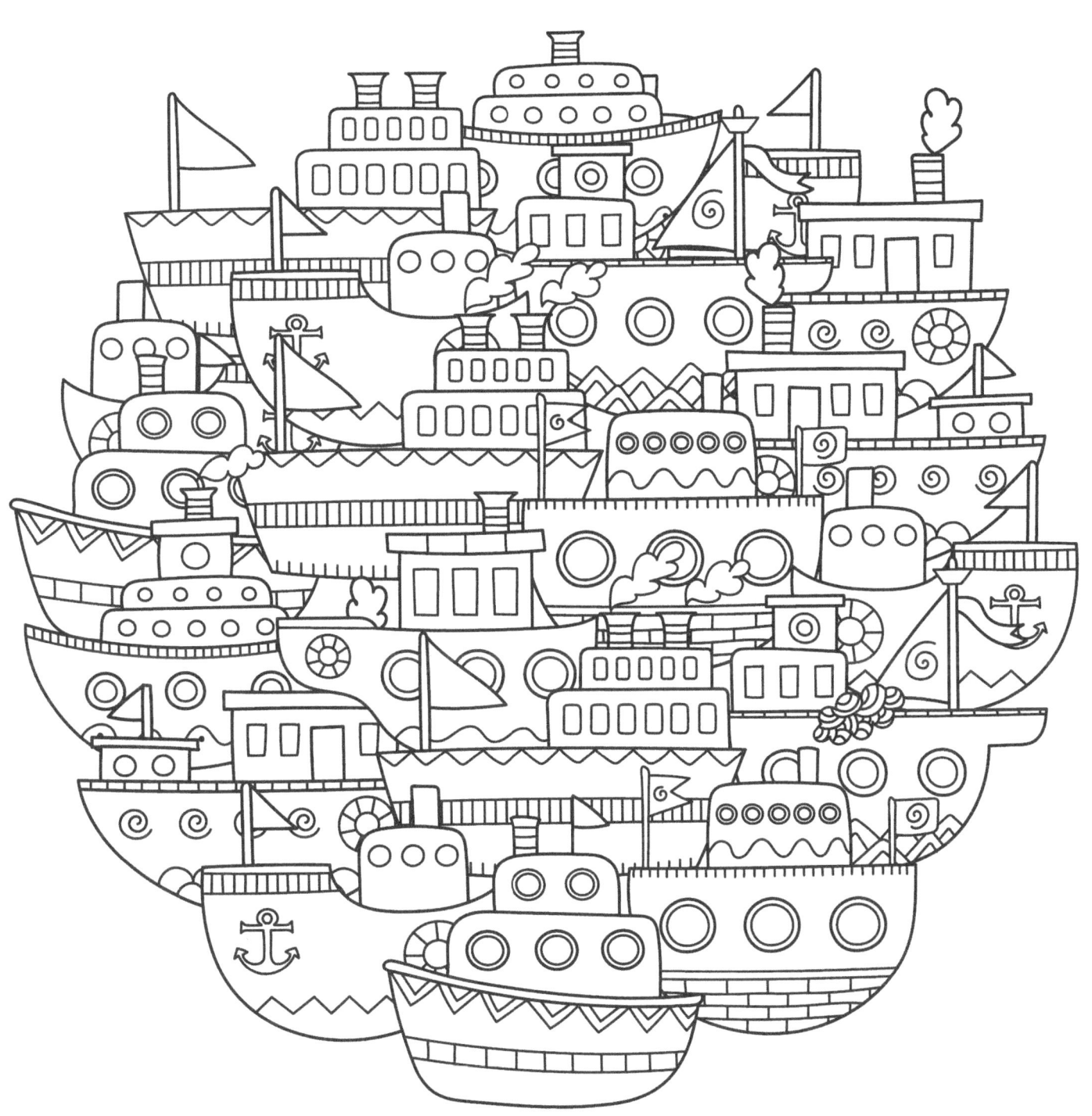

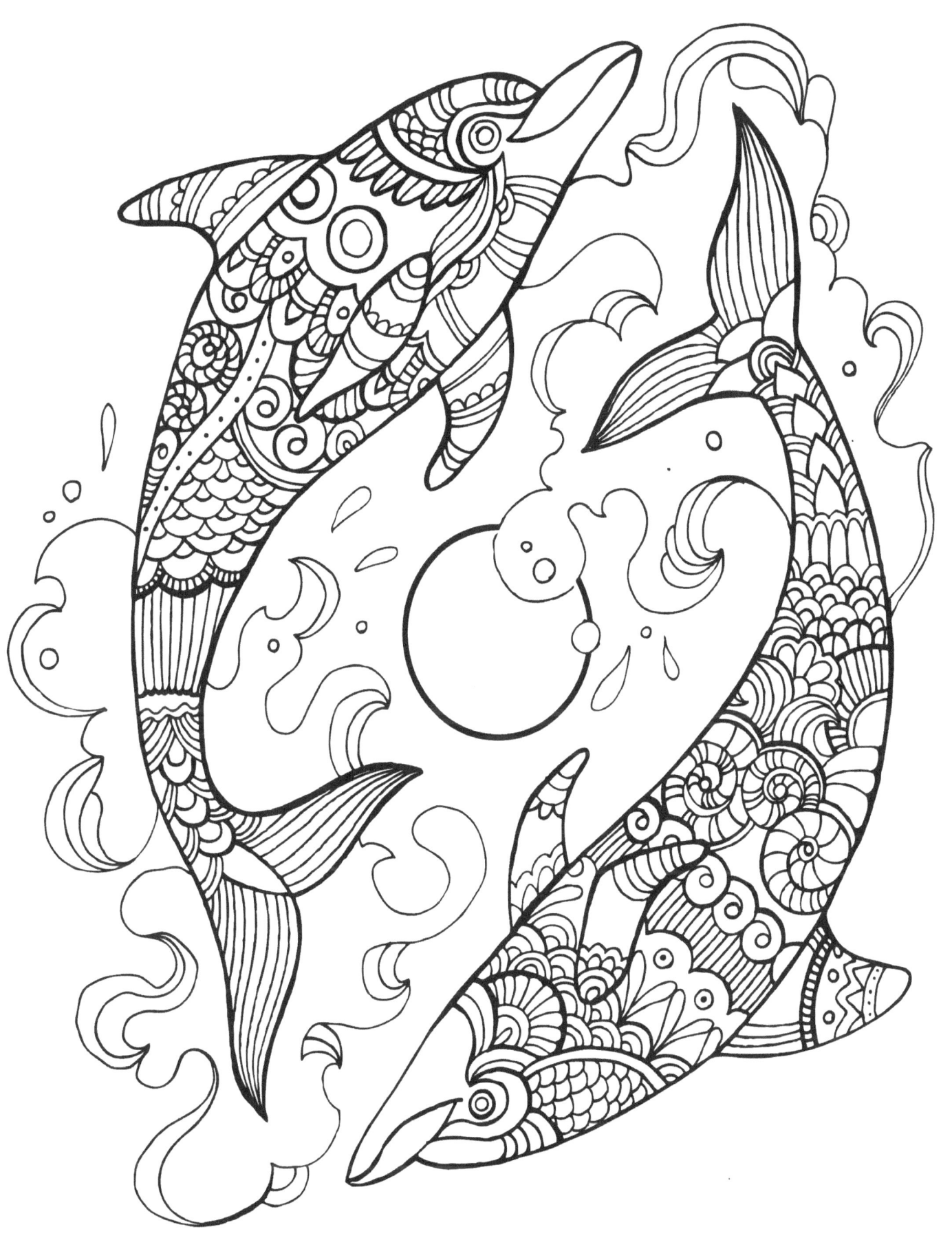

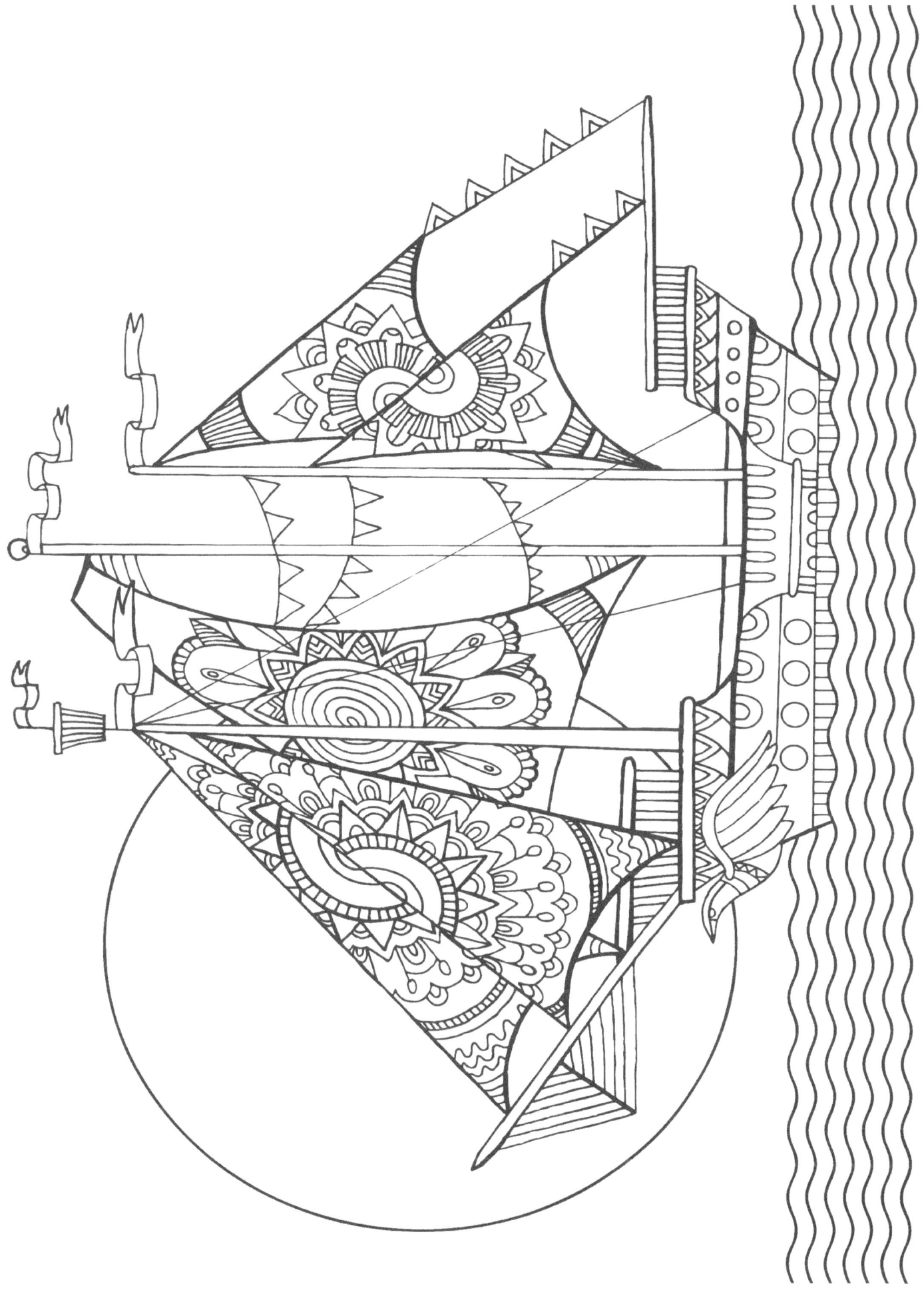

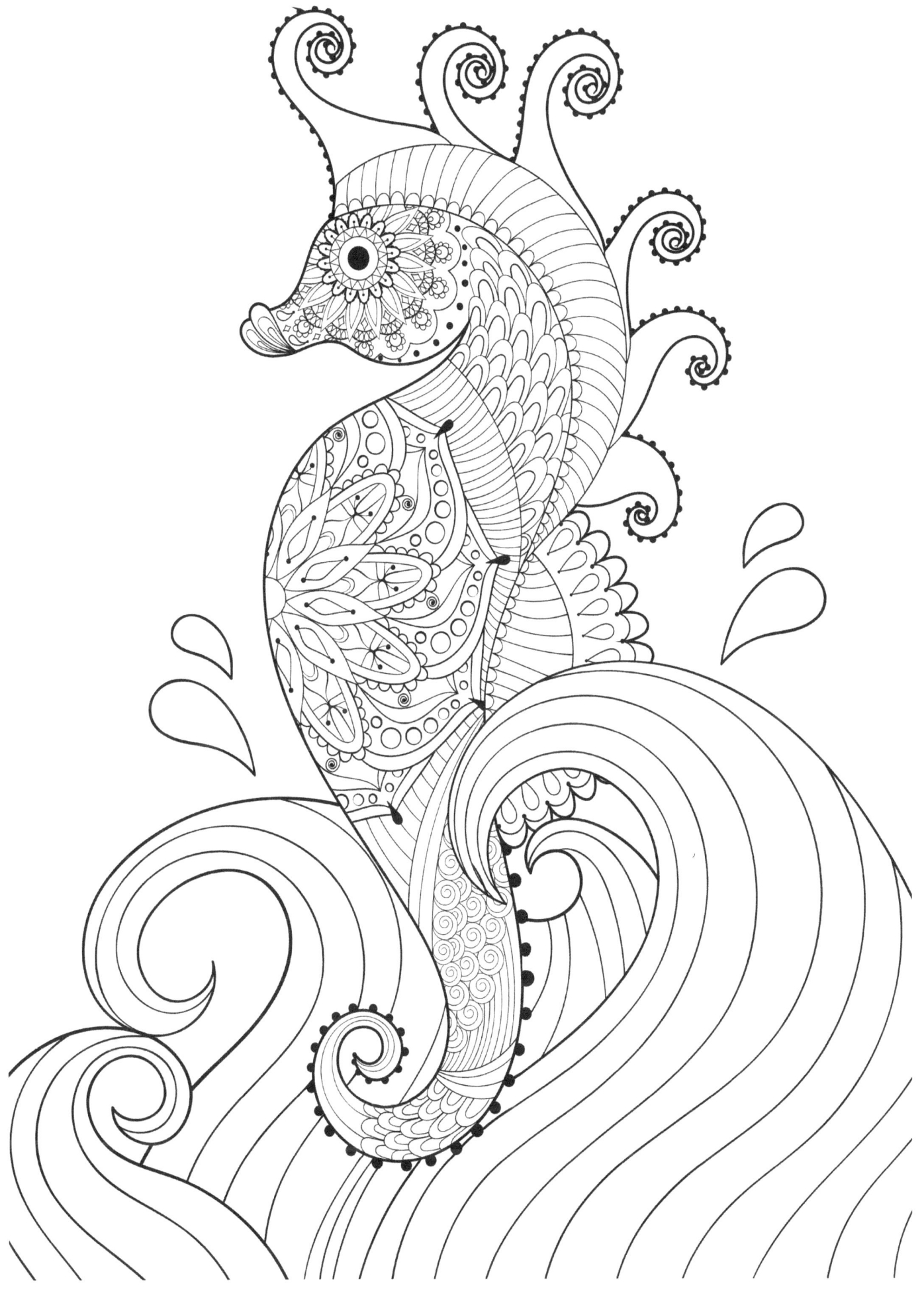

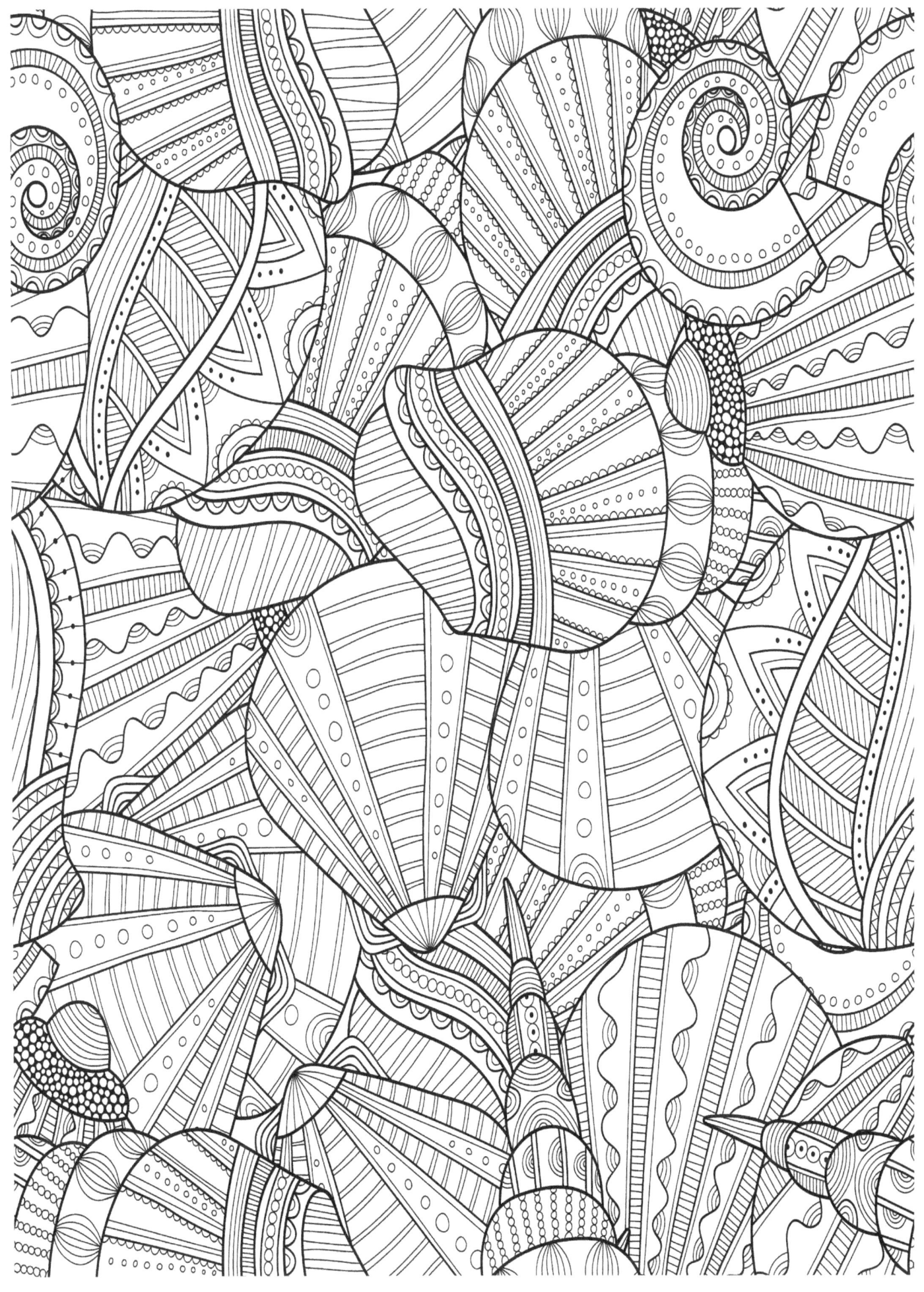

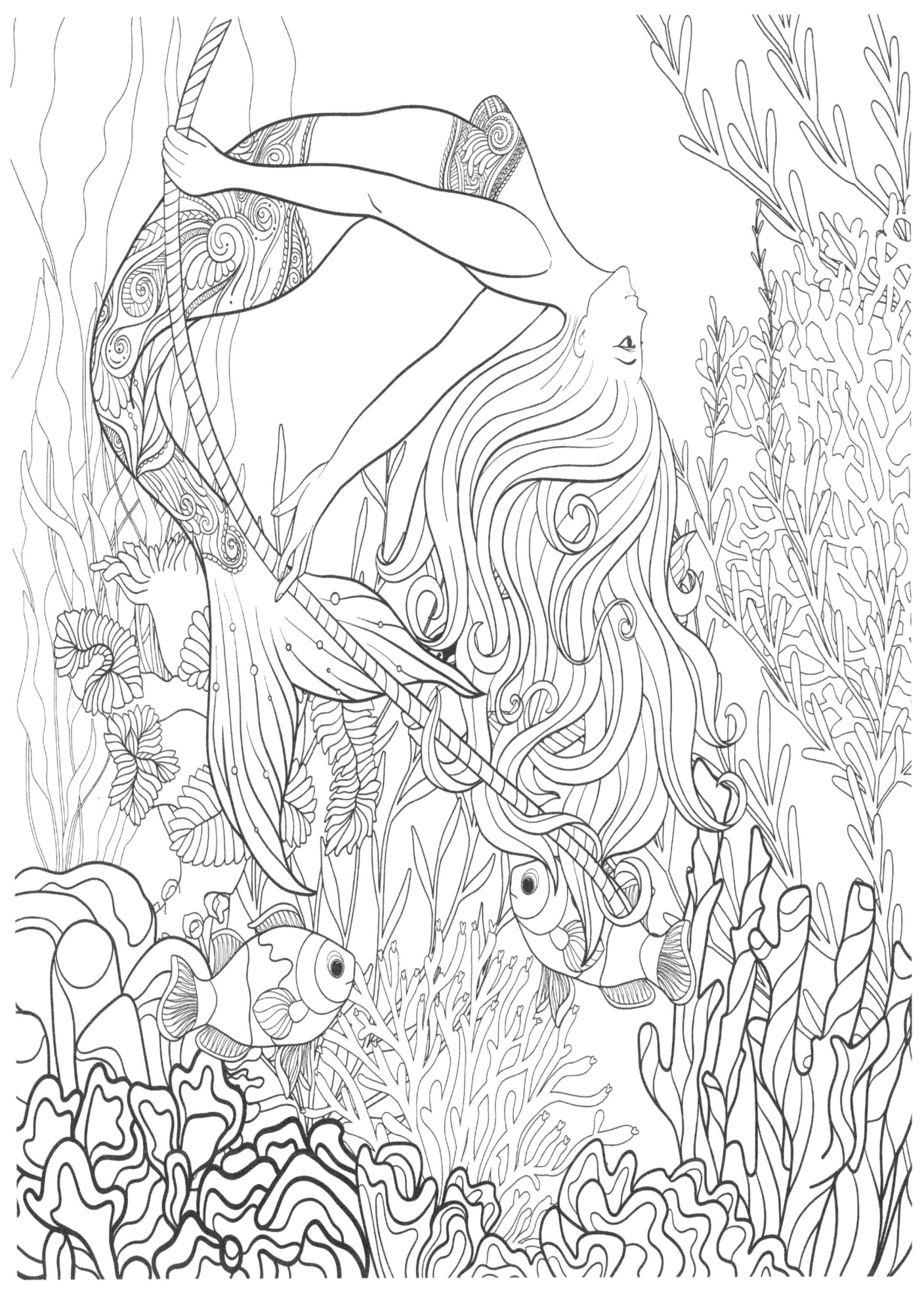

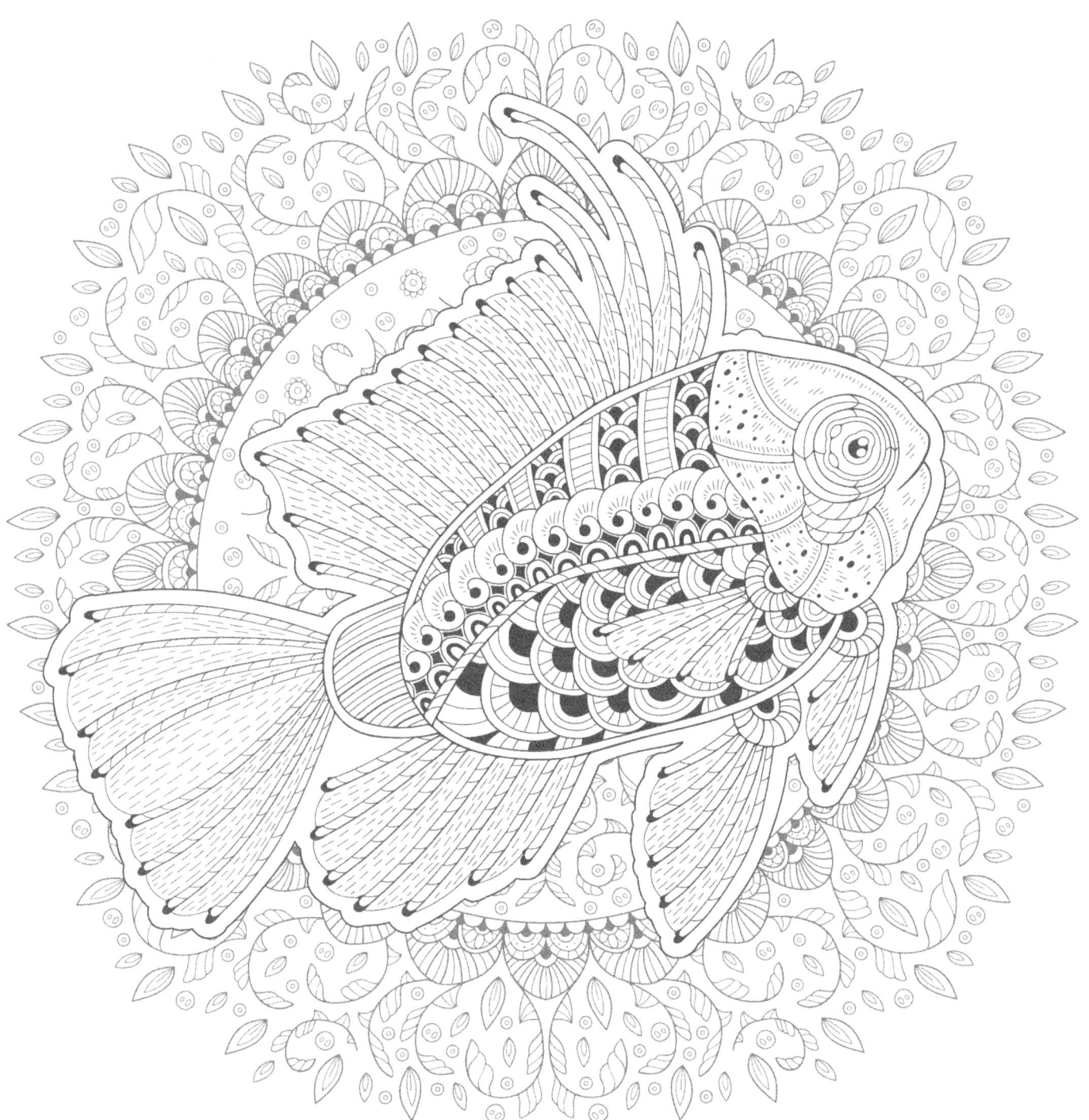

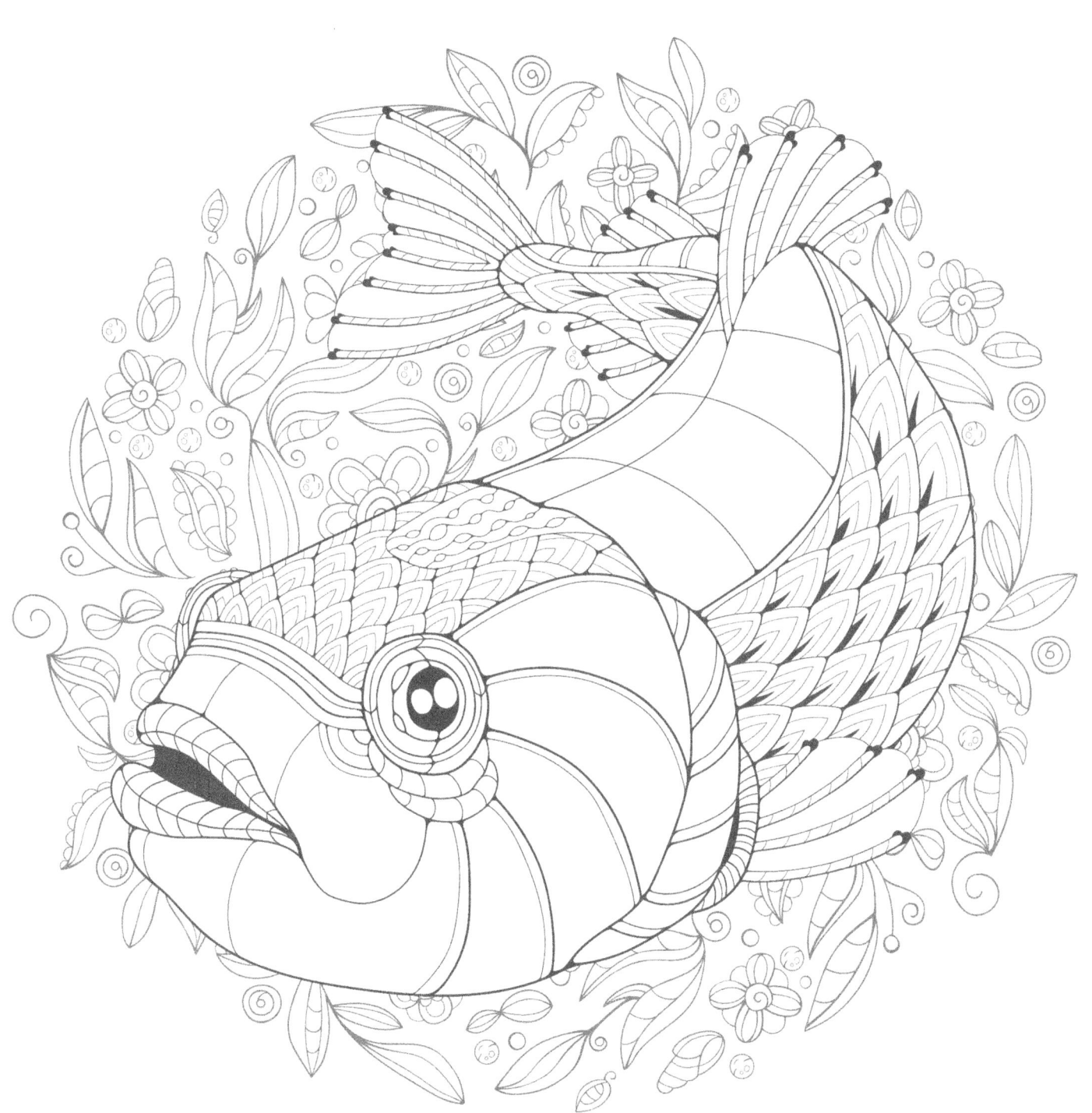

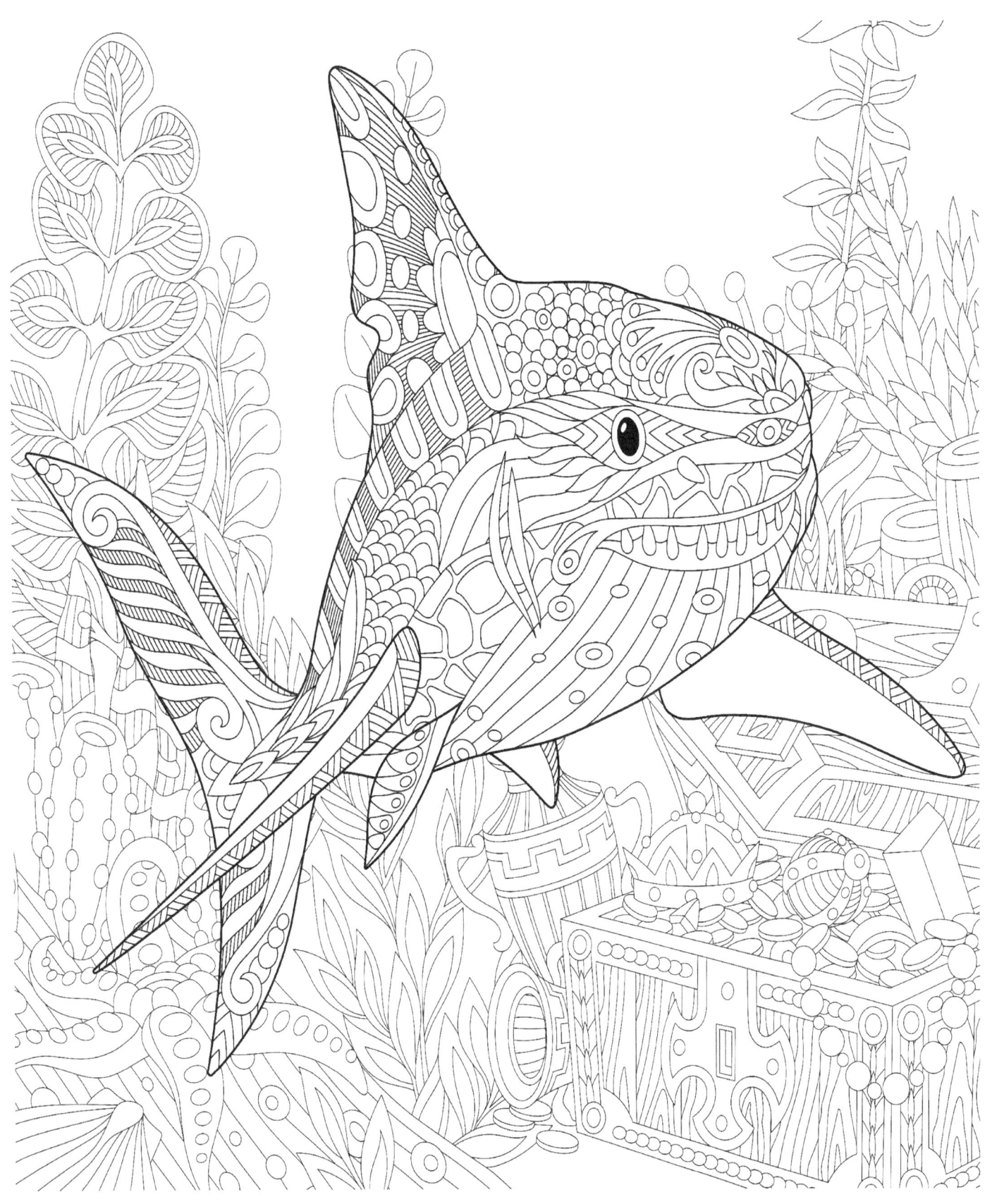

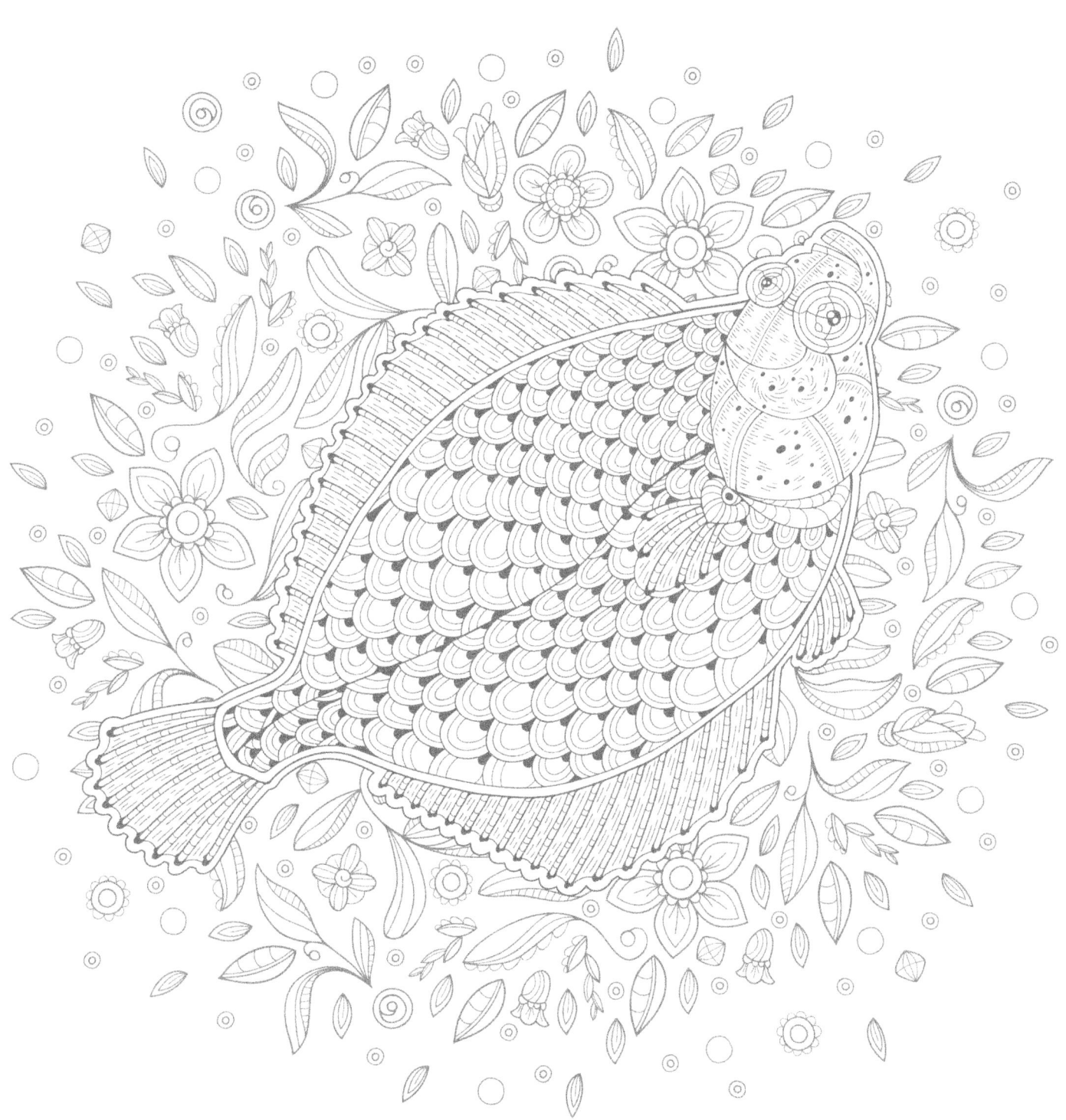

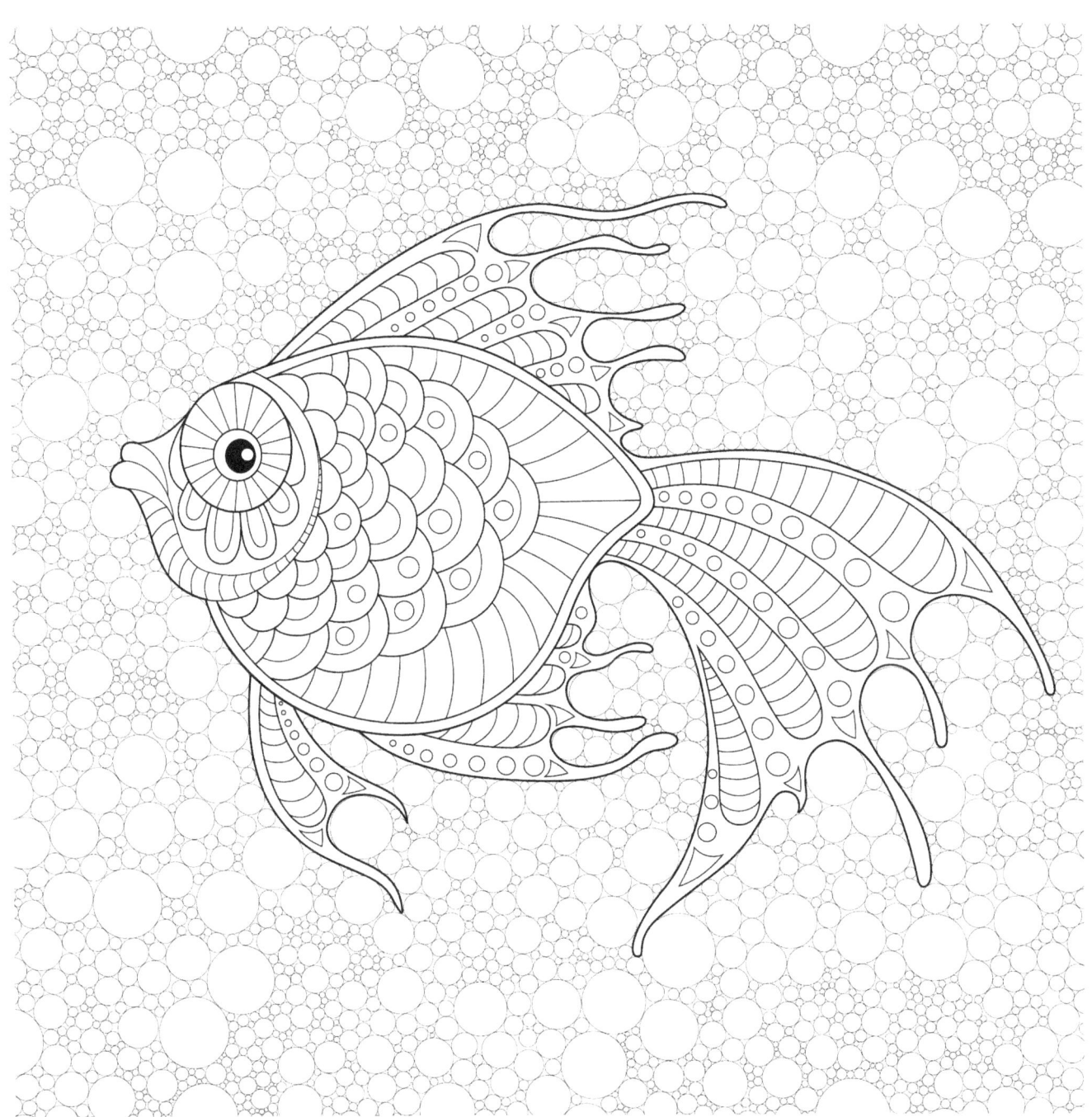

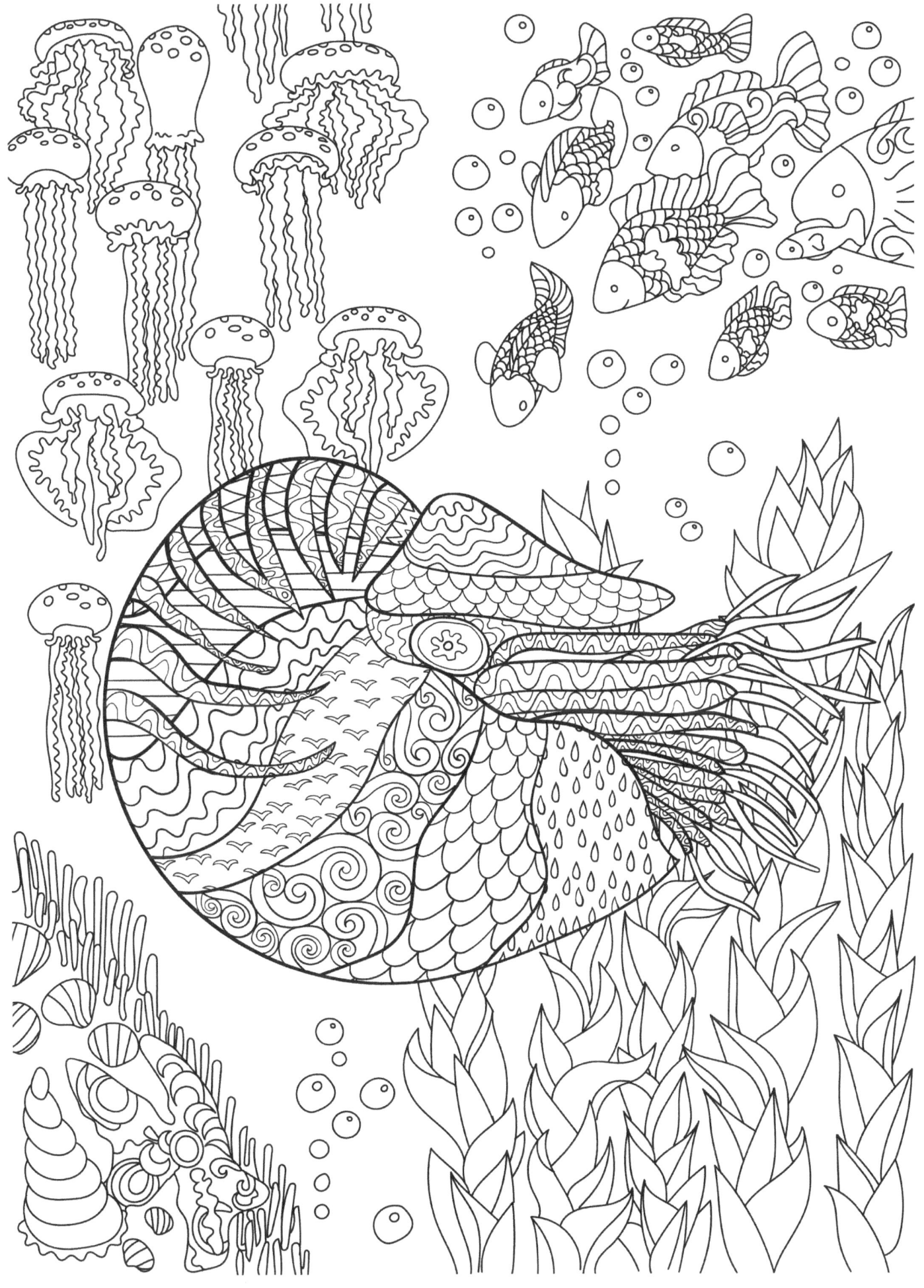

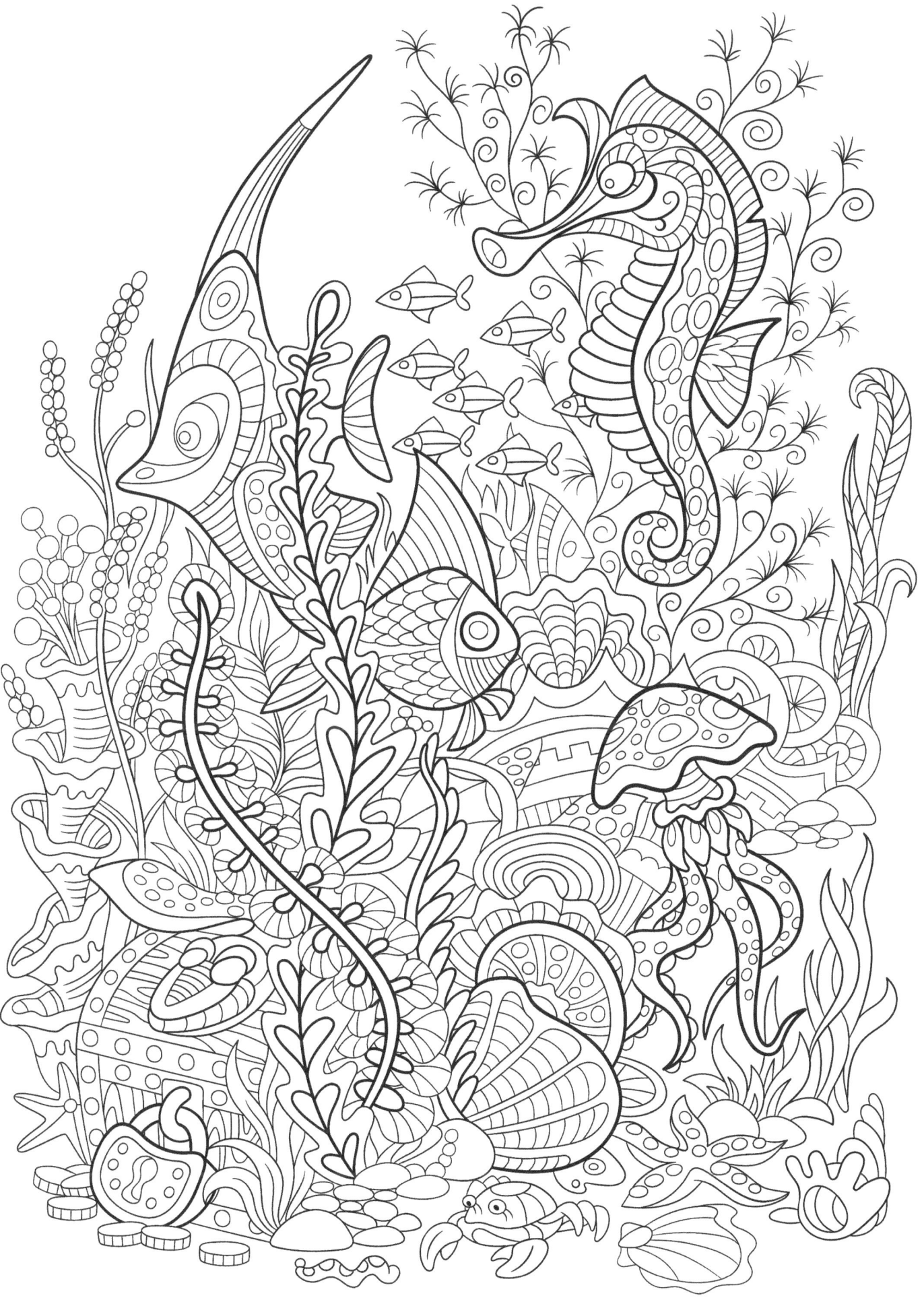

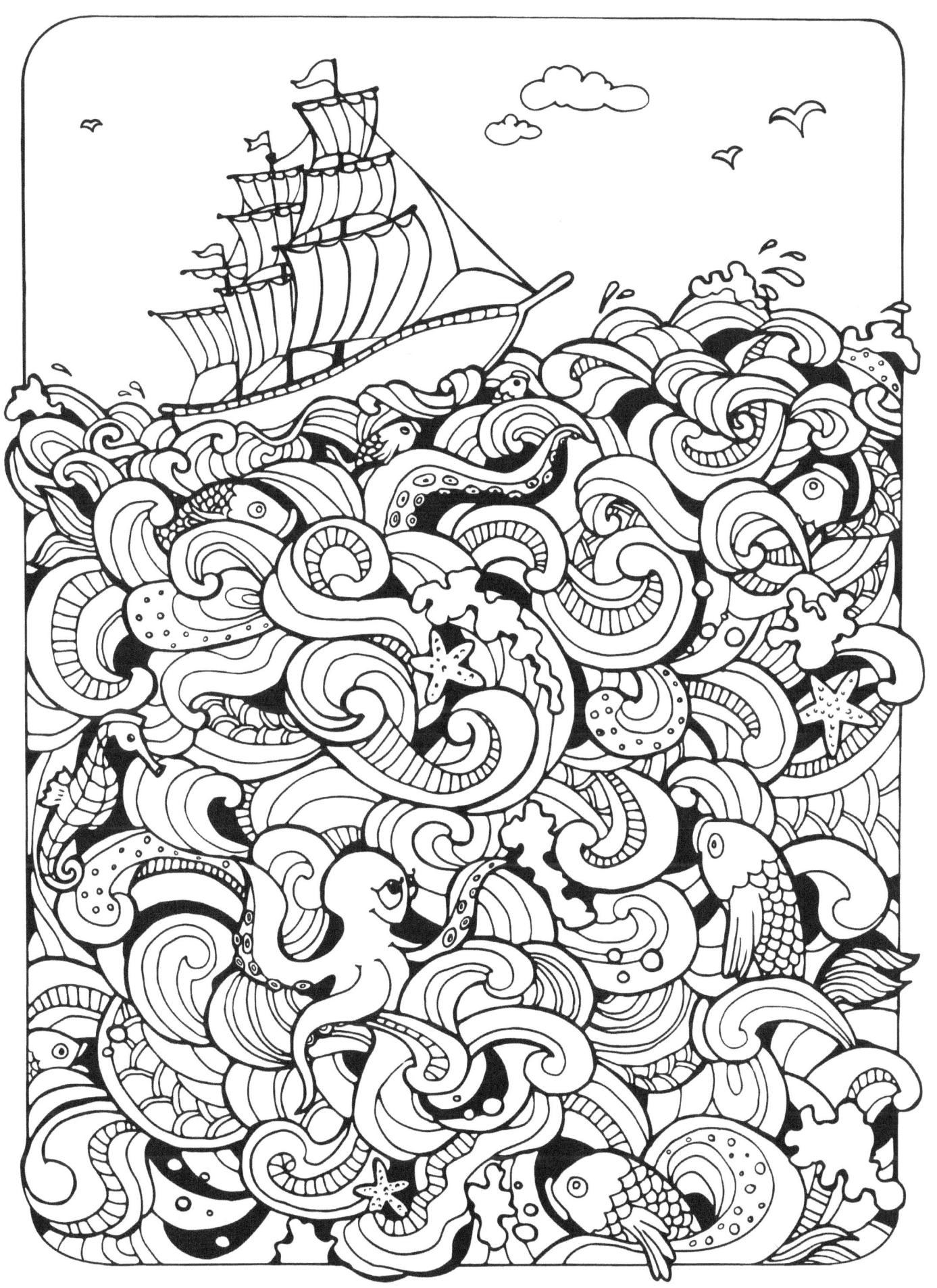

www.ingramcontent.com/pod-product-compliance
Lightning Source LLC
Chambersburg PA
CBHW080530220526
45465CB00006B/2655